There's a God in My Closet

There's a God in My Closet

*Encountering the Love
Who Embraces Our Skeletons*

BEN DeLONG
Foreword by Brad Jersak

RESOURCE *Publications* · Eugene, Oregon

To Irene, my constant companion on this journey.
I would not be where I am without you.

To my late Grandpa Green. The love and affection you lavished
made us feel infinitely valuable, just as Jesus's Abba does.
Your grace-filled presence will never be forgotten.

THE GOD IN MY CLOSET

A long time ago, my skeletons were screwing things up for me.

They'd pop out of the closet at the most inopportune times and thwart my best plans.

So I decided to solve the problem once and for all.

I locked them away in my closet, inside cabinets, and chests, and safes.

They were out of the way, and I mostly forgot they were there.

But one day, I heard noise coming from inside the closet.

It was disturbing, and frightening, and unexpected.

I leaned in, and to my horror, realized that God was in my closet.

I heard condemnation and retribution.

I tried to ignore it, hoping this scary entity would go away, or at least never come out to see me.

I knew him to be harsh and unpredictable, one who battered his own son, and tortured my soul at every mistake and wrong turn.

Over time the noise became so distracting that I couldn't focus on anything else.

The ruckus was worse than ever, so I resolved to face God and tell him to leave.

When I opened the door, however, I was astonished at what I found.

God was sitting down at a table, chatting with my skeletons.

They were dining together, laughing, and enjoying each other's company.

I wasn't sure if I should be frightened or embarrassed.

Then God turned and gave me a monumental smile.

"You've finally come!" He exclaimed, as he waved me over to the table.

"Come sit with me, I'd like you to meet my friends."

Contents

Permissions

Falling Upward by Richard Rhor, Copyright © 2011 by Richard Rhor. All rights reserved. Used by permission of Wiley. Published by Jossey-Bass, A Wiley Imprint www.josseybass.com

The Illumined Heart by Frederica Mathewes-Greene. Copyright © 2001 by Frederica Mathewes-Greene. Used by permission of Paraclete Press. www.paraclete-press.com

The Orthodox Way by Kalistos Ware. Copyright © 1979 by Kalistos Ware. Used by permission of St Vladimir's Seminary Press. www.svspress.com

Finding Church by Wayne Jacobsen. Copyright ©2014 by Wayne Jacobsen. Used by permission of Lifestream. www.lifestream.org

What is the Bible by Rob Bell. *Reprinted by permission of HarperCollins Publishers Ltd.* © *2017 Rob Bell*

Foreword

CLOSETS.

Closets: cupboards, cabinets, cloakrooms. These have never been benign for me. From childhood, they were dark places—hiding places. A place where dark things hid and where I hid dark things. Phrases such as "skeletons in my closet" and "coming out of the closet" didn't emerge from nowhere. Closets were the secret forts of stolen kisses, the vaults where you stashed your *Kiss* records, the lair where scary spirits lurked. Closets were where you hide stuff from parents and from God.

But when "God" is one of the frightening monsters in your closet, you know you're in deep doo-doo. That's one thing Ben DeLong and I have in common. I resonate with his dual description of (a) the ugly images of monster-God in the closet and (b) the healing we experience when the true God—Jesus Christ—is allowed in.

I actually began with a relatively healthy connection to Christ. My parents were largely healthy representatives of the God who loves us and revealed himself through Jesus. I remember loving and trusting Jesus Christ as my originary default mode. Jesus was, for me, good news—a faithful Nightlight in the darkness.

But that Light was distorted into "strange fire" at about the age of eight. It was a combination of fear-filled hellfire evangelism and dispensational "left behind" teaching. I did enjoy some level of immunity because in our tradition, those who said the "sinner's prayer" were assured that we were safe—permanently. Even if you fell off the wagon by "backsliding," you were safe. Well, you were safe *if* you had really said the prayer sincerely from the heart . . . and backsliding indicated that maybe you hadn't. So, every slip was cause for second-guessing.

The ominous threat of hell entered the picture for me at Bible camp. A group of third-graders sit around a growing teepee fire as our counselor quickly swipes his hand through the flames. Then in his best ghost-story voice, he asks, "What if you held your hand there for a minute? How about an hour? How about your whole body . . . for ever and ever!"

Who knows what he said next, but it led to an invitation to pray the Prayer and be saved from God's eternal rotisserie. Who wouldn't? I already had. But the threat was real for me, nonetheless, because I imagined all my "unsaved loved ones"—my beloved cousins and aunties and uncles— screaming in never-ending torment as their skin and nerve endings burned without ever being consumed. Not only that: unless I converted them, their blood, I was told, would be on my hands. Whatever that's supposed to mean.

Add to that Hal Lindsay's popular rapture theology and the specter of Armageddon. In my church, we were assured that all believers would be caught up into heaven before "the Great Tribulation." If we just said the Prayer, we wouldn't be "left behind" (I think the best response to this is the Simpson's episode "Left Below"). This was the era of the Cold War and the Battle of Yom Kippur. I was excited to think that within a week or two, the Lord would be coming to get me. No such luck.

Though I was supposedly "in," every time my parents were home late from work and no one would answer their business lines, the left-behind monster would bite me, and I'd be repenting on my face until they showed up. The whole theological system was very real and traumatizing and abusive. Monster-god indeed.

✦

The story of how that all unraveled is long and complex. And it is Ben's turn to tell it. But I will share one event that illustrates the journey back to sanity.

As a rookie youth minister, I chose to keep my evangelism to teens simple and clean: "God loves you." That should keep me out of trouble. It didn't.

One day, a girl named Terri-Ann came for prayer. She asked, "You said God loves me. Well then, where was God when I was a latch-key kid, tiptoe-ing through used syringes in the trailer court, terrified and locking myself in until my parents got home?"

Good question. For her, God was not nasty. He was just an absent, a deadbeat dad in the sky, not there when she needed him. I responded: "I think you should ask him."

She prayed loudly, "Where were you!??"—more of an accusation than a question. Then she burst into tears, fled my office and raced off down the sidewalk into the dark night.

I'm fired, I thought. *Or sued . . .*

Heather, the youth sponsor who had brought Terri to see me, spoke up:

"I just saw a picture of her in my mind. She was hiding in a closet in the trailer. I saw Jesus holding her and rocking her. Do you think I should go after her?"

"I wish you would," I pleaded.

So Heather rushed out of my office in hot pursuit. I either prayed or mentally prepared my resignation letter . . . I don't remember. But in a few minutes, Terri and Heather both reappeared. Heather was glowing and Terri was still crying, but now with tears of joy!

"What happened?"

Heather began, "As I chased Terri down the street, she was already laughing and dancing her way back here! You won't believe what happened . . ."

"He was in the closet!" Terri blurted. "Jesus reminded me that I used to hide in the closet and just rock myself for comfort. But I wasn't alone. He was with me the whole time! Holding me close and rocking me to peace in the closet!"

That was my introduction to inner healing in 1990. God was no longer the monster in the closet, but the one who comes to the darkest and loneliest of our closets to hold and heal us. That's where this book is taking us. Enjoy the journey!

BRAD JERSAK
Author of *A More Christlike God*
On the Feast of Maximos the Confessor

Acknowledgments

It is difficult to thank everyone who had a hand in this book. This book flows out of who I am, and I would not know who I am without the presence and love of so many people. I want to thank my parents. They have loved me dearly, and shielded us kids from cycles in their families of origin. The older I get and experience life as an adult, the more thankful I am for them. They and my three sisters mean so much to me.

So many people have helped in my healing process. Dr. Paul Fitzgerald and his wife Susanna have been a wonderful mentoring presence in our lives. Their Breakthrough seminar was a catalyst for so much of my journey. As soon as I met them, I knew I wanted the inner peace and contentment that they so obviously enjoyed. Father Tom, my spiritual director, has been pivotal in helping me understand faith in a healthier and more faithful way. Tom Darcy's therapeutic presence has helped me to work through so many barriers that have kept me from living loved. Joan Turner, Curt Waddle, Michael Palmer: your friendships gave me a safe place to express concerns and doubts when I didn't know how to trust myself. Most of all, my amazing wife Irene. You have believed in me and encouraged me every step of the way. I am so thankful for your loving presence. I am a very blessed man! If not for all these people (and so many more), I would not know the power of Christ's love and the transforming impact it has had in my life.

There have also been many who have helped me with this writing project. Curt Waddle, Donnie Miller, Monte Asbury, Josh Broward, and Luke Allison all gave me invaluable feedback. Janet Chaniot gave so much time to help me edit the book. I can't thank her enough! Also, a huge thank you to Brad Jersak for writing the forward, not to mention the impact his own writings have had on me.

I could keep going for a while, but I will leave it at that. Thank you all so much!

Introduction

"CAN YOU PLEASE STOP asking me that all the time? It's getting annoying."

I know my sister meant well, but she was always assuming something was wrong with me. I was fine, for the most part. Besides, talking about it wouldn't do any good. Nobody really understood me anyway. I had gotten along just fine keeping everything to myself. That would eventually change. My sister wouldn't be the last person to see the pain on my face, and to ask repeatedly, "What's wrong?" I could only keep it under wraps for so long. Our crap tends to come out one way or another.

It would eventually come out as depression and anxiety, which are an all too common presence in our society. I can now personally vouch for that. It wasn't always that way though. For so much of my life, church and faith were the entities that protected me from such afflictions.

Church was a safe haven for me growing up, at least the way I understood it back then. I wasn't picked on at school, nor was I part of the in crowd. At church it was different. I felt cool, even admired there. I suppose part of that was from being a pastor's kid and being perceived as super religious.

It wasn't just a reputation, either. I took my faith seriously. I went to church every chance I had. I prayed often. I read my Bible as much as I could, routinely taking it to study hall to pass time. My best moments were at church camp and with my youth group friends.

My faith protected me and provided a neat and tidy way of seeing the world. There was a clear sense of what was right and wrong as well as the rewards and punishments for each. We knew who was in and who was out. And of course, we were in.

As a teenager, it was a good way to approach things. It made sense to me. If there was a monster in my closet, God was the one who kept it at bay.

As I grew up, left for college, and became an adult, things became less simple and straightforward. I encountered questions I had never even imagined when I was younger. Inner struggles, pain, and anxiety were rising up inside me. They were realities which were always there, but up until that time I had ignored them. Perhaps I just hadn't been forced to face them.

Eventually, I was reeling from deep insecurity and depression and was confronted with a difficult truth. The God I had learned to follow was not as warm and fuzzy as we made him out to be. He was like a bully: great to have on your side, but objectively not a very comforting presence. My emotional and spiritual lives were becoming unstable. I had to admit there was a monster in my closet, and it was God.

The only way for me to break through to the other side was to enter the closet and face what was holding me back. When I entered in, however, what I discovered was unexpected to say the least. It was more difficult than I would have imagined, and yet lighter than what I was leaving behind. This book is about my journey to something new, something real, something excruciatingly confrontational, but ultimately something for my good. This book is about a question. What do you do when the faith and beliefs that were supposed to bring you joy and peace become the source of your anxiety and depression?

PART I

FOLLOWING THE PAIN CRUMBS

CHAPTER 1

The Depressed Elephant in the Room

I'M JUST GOING TO say it; life sucks sometimes. At times that's all we can really say. We believe somehow it should be better. Somehow people shouldn't be able to get away with being jerks (including myself), our family and friends shouldn't get cancer, and children shouldn't be facing life without enough food or clean water.

But these things happen, and it sucks. Even with decent parents raising us, we can still end up scarred and broken. Most of us didn't have parents who intentionally tried to screw us up. I can't imagine my parents ever sitting around thinking, "I wonder what we could do to Ben that would make a counselor a lot of money someday." My parents love me and always have. That's the case for most people, with some glaring and terrible exceptions. Even loving parents can leave scars, though. They often can't see how their own insecurities and hang-ups influence the way they handle life and impact those around them. So we can end up with our own scars in the midst of good intentions.

Life can really suck, due to many different reasons, and often due to no one's intended fault. I think we all understand that quite well. I was told, however, that there was a remedy for this, something that would take the sting away. And that something, or someone, was Jesus. The way many of us were taught to follow Jesus and to do life, however, eventually left something to be desired.

I was essentially taught that if I went to church, listened to the right music, read my Bible everyday, and surrounded myself with church people, then everything would essentially work out okay. The ugly truth that was often left out was that sometimes church people can do all these things and still be left depressed and bitter. Sometimes they can also be assholes (including me).

Now of course, when I say everything would work out okay, I don't mean we expected everything to go smoothly. We were reminded often that "no one ever said it would be easy." But we were assured that the joy we would experience would be incomparable. We were promised a peace that would be beyond our understanding. We were told of a love that conquers all.

The trouble came when those things didn't seem to show up very often, if at all. Most of the time we just assumed we were lacking in our faith. After all, the Bible was supposed to be our instruction manual. If we can't put the new product together, it's usually because we're not following directions very well. For example, Paul tells us in Philippians that if we pray with thanksgiving, we will experience peace. Thus, when we don't experience the peace that Paul speaks of, we look over the instructions again and wonder, "Am I praying right? Am I really rejoicing always and being thankful?" It feels like an impossible standard. It is in the Bible, however, so we naturally assume we are lacking something.

Jesus seemed pretty generous in his promises, though. He doesn't seem like the kind of guy who would skimp on our blessings because we forgot to dot a couple i's. He claimed to bring life abundantly. He even advertised that his yoke was easy and his burden was light. It doesn't seem as though he was requiring a degree in rocket science to experience what he believed.

Yet, I seemed to be lacking that life most of the time. I wasn't experiencing peace or joy, and I definitely didn't know much about unconditional love. I ended up depressed, anxious, and incredibly insecure.

Life sucks sometimes. I get it. But my faith was not resolving any of my deep spiritual and emotional afflictions of depression, anxiety, and the like. In fact, it was making them much, much worse. And in some instances, my faith was actually causing them.

There was a big elephant in the room: I was depressed, and in many cases my underlined Bible was practically drawing the frown across my face. Eventually, I had to confront something incredibly difficult. My faith was not working. It was not coming through as promised. If I was going to experience what my heart truly longed for, I would need to give it up.

STANDING UP TO THE MONSTER

When I was a teenager, I used to play baseball by myself in our backyard. I grew up in northern Iowa, where the nose hairs freeze in the winter and the beads of sweat flow in the summer. Just a couple swings of the bat in the sweltering summer were enough to wet my forehead. It was an elaborate event in my head. I would keep track of stats or have home run derbies. All the while I made sure I had the batting stance correct for the player I was impersonating. I was very adept at entertaining myself.

One summer, I concocted the perfect ball. It was a foam ball wrapped in a thick layer of duct tape. The tape allowed the ball to have a little weight to it but not so much that it would break a window. It remains, to this day, one of my greatest inventions.

One day, however, I was unable to find my specially crafted baseball. My only option was a ball that was made of hard plastic. "This shouldn't be able to break a window," I assured myself. So I ventured, somewhat reluctantly, out in the backyard to play.

I think my first few swings were unimpressive. A miss here. A foul there. It took a bit to get used to the new ball, but once I did, I jolted it. But as I was looking on triumphantly at my connection, I heard the dreaded sound: breaking glass.

My life flashed before my eyes. The house was a huge source of stress for my dad. He was a pastor, and we lived in the house owned by the church. Anything that happened to the house was seemingly a threat to his job and our livelihood.

Fortunately, he was not home when the catastrophe occurred. I ran to the house to assess the damage. At the time we had two panels for each window, and fortunately the main one was still intact. I convened with my mom immediately. She decided that, considering the unobservant nature of my dad (that's where I get that from), we could just knock out the rest of the broken glass and close the main window without him noticing.

That worked for a while, for months even. But one day my dad was messing with the window and stumbled upon our secret. I did the only thing I could think of: run to my mom. I knew that she would stand up for me.

This is a pretty accurate representation of the way I approached my faith for much of my life. I ran to Jesus to protect me from the Father. There was a key difference, though. My earthly father might have yelled at me if I did something wrong. God, on the other hand, was apparently not opposed to extreme measures of punishment. I could never really anticipate the way God the Father was going to interact with me. Sure, he sent his Son for us. But if I was to believe that all of scripture was equally accurate, he was also a pretty volatile personality. We never know what we're going to get with him. Sometimes he's showering mercy; other times he's commanding genocide. Sometimes he's comforting the religious outcast who just can't seem to measure up; other times he's striking people dead for inadvertently breaking the rules.

In the afterlife, God's character gets more concerning. Those on his good side are accepted. The meaning of being on God's good side is somewhat mysterious in the understanding many Christians have of the Gospel, but I'll get into that later. Even if we are included in the (seemingly) few who get in, we are still dealing with a God who treats the outsiders with an uncomfortable level of ferocity. Is God really going to throw sinners into a lake of fire? If that punishment was reserved for people like mass murderers, it would be a little more understandable. According to the Gospel that is often proclaimed by many Christians, however, it's also going to be someone's sweet Grandma, or loyal brother. It will be people who often are the epitome of compassion and kindness, but who simply could not bring themselves to confess believing in a God they could not see.

Some readers may be in sync with me. Others, no doubt, are uncomfortable with what appear to be sacrilegious questions. If you are the latter, I can assure you that in the past I would have been uncomfortable as well. The main point of being a Christian, however, is to live like Jesus. I don't mean that we can be perfect and never make mistakes but, simply, that our lives can revolve around love, compassion, and truth as Jesus's life did. I grew up within a tribe of Christianity that believes this is possible. The problem is that the Gospel we proclaim often has God telling us to love him, or to refuse and be tortured by him. That doesn't sound inviting. Frankly, that sounds more like the plot to a movie about an abusive husband. At the end of the day, that narrative doesn't help me live like Jesus. Instead it brings up fear and anger. I can't trust a God like that.

This is a pivotal problem in the evangelical community, in my experience. We are told to cast all of our anxiety on God, to let him comfort and redirect us. God is supposed to be the one person we can run to when we screw up. When I have messed up, however, God has often been the last person I would turn to. He throws sinners into the lake of fire; what's stopping him from doing the same to me? The way to peace is to run to God in times of trouble and failure, but his volatile nature often led me to run the opposite direction.

Many Christians, and others who are interested in faith, are very concerned about the God who is often portrayed in our gospel narrative. They believe there is something bigger. They see the benefit of faith in their lives or the lives of others, but something keeps nagging at them. How do we trust a God who so often seems two-faced in his behavior? How do we honor a God who seems prone to violence when that is the very behavior that is tearing our world apart?

There is a pivotal point to understand in all this. When people question the God we often teach and worship, many who love church and this faith can be offended. To them it feels like blasphemy to ask these kinds of questions. They might conclude that people are only asking these questions because we are being influenced by others. Or perhaps we are simply accessing our sentimental feelings and are ignoring the matter of justice. Here's the distinction that needs to be made: There is no doubt that our inner voice, as well as exposure to other ideas, has influence on us. But the main reason Christians are asking these questions is Jesus himself. We cannot accept a portrait of a God who is temperamental and prone to violence when Jesus is the one who teaches us to love our enemies. This Jesus is the one who cries for forgiveness as he dies in front of his accusers. We need a faith that is honest and faithful to the Son of God we claim to worship.

This is also an important issue for those who are outside of faith looking in. There are many who love the teachings of Jesus and are profoundly moved by the love and compassion he demonstrated. However, they cannot accept him if he comes in a package deal with a violent and temperamental Father. They can't accept a God who would annihilate or torture the majority of the human race because they didn't believe the right things. Nor can they accept a God who commands genocide based on what a tribe's ancestors did. Many Christians assume atheists and agnostics are rejecting faith. In reality, they often simply have the same concerns Jesus seemed to have.

Eventually these became my concerns as well. This faith I was living in nurtured my shame. I believed there was inherently something wrong with me, irredeemable even. The evangelical gospel was there quickly to confirm it. I learned that God didn't like me very much. Sure, he loved me in a "you're my kid, I have to love you" sort of way. Deep down, however, he was so displeased with me that he couldn't stand to look in my direction. His sense of purity would not allow him to.

Of course, we are complicated beings, and are impacted by our experiences in many different ways. Therefore, my inner tensions do not solely stem from my faith. Part of my shame came from absorbing my dad's stress from church and, when he acted out of that stress, assuming it was a reflection on me. Children often rely on an idealized image of their parents. When a parent acts in a way that doesn't fit the part, the child will often assume it is his fault in order to hold onto the idealized image. My dad was simply human and therefore imperfect, but I assumed any imperfection was because of me. And, to be clear, I love both my parents very much and am incredibly thankful for them.

My opinion of my father wasn't the only one that mattered, however. The church's opinion of my dad as the pastor, and us as his representatives, was paramount as well. Thus, much of my shame came from church life in general and from being chastised when I did not fit the "good little pastor's son" mold.

The psychological effect of these issues was significant. I came to believe that I was defective, that I didn't belong. My dad would never have intentionally made me feel that way, but when we are young certain experiences affect us in deep ways and tag along like an unwelcome traveling companion.

My companion arrived when, from a very early age, I took in a sense of rejection and disdain for myself. My life became one attempt after another to fix it. I became the dutiful religious servant and, over time, the model child. Unfortunately, none of my efforts seemed to change anything.

As the emotional tornado of my teen years struck, I saw in the beauty of girls another way to ease my suffering. If I could just find a girl that thought I was special and worth loving, I was sure I would be whole again. With each girlfriend a new hope arose in me. A temporary confidence and relief would flood my inner being only to be ripped away when the worst was confirmed: you're not special, not wanted, not worth it.

As painful as those experiences were, the pain would become more intense when I left home and became an adult. I went to college to pursue being a pastor. I definitely had a sense that God was calling me to ministry, but looking back I can see that my shame had a hand in it as well. Becoming a pastor was yet another option to soothe my pain and get God off my back. For a while it worked. I found out that I was more intelligent than I thought. I was earning straight A's and finding a niche. Most importantly, however, I met a fascinating girl while I worked washing dishes in the cafeteria.

The dish room was not the most pleasant place to be. It was hot, cluttered, and boring. The plates and bowls revolving around the corner seemed never to end, but Irene made it better. I felt so comfortable around her. I was not a very outgoing teenager by any means, but with her it was different. Initially she was even annoyed at how much I talked. We became friends, and eventually I asked her out on our first date.

She told me her four digit phone extension, but I didn't have a pen to write it down. The whole way back to my dorm room I just kept reciting it, over and over, to make sure I would not forget. "3752, 3752, 3752." It's a good thing I didn't have to remember seven digits!

We were quickly taken with each other. We could talk with ease, sharing deep pains and thoughts we had seldom shared with anyone else. We would sit on the bleachers or find a bench somewhere to kiss and talk until it was time to return to our claustrophobic dorm rooms. We grossed out our friends on more than one occasion.

Although I knew very soon that I wanted to marry her, I waited until our one year anniversary to propose. I wrote her a song, and a close friend helped me make a proposal video where I trekked through fields and neighborhoods toward her dorm building, all to the tune of "500 Miles." Yeah, I got game. Twenty one months later we were taking pictures on a steamy June day, preparing to share our vows. My dream had finally come true. I had found a beautiful girl to love me, who believed I was special. I belonged to her.

It didn't take long, however, for a difficult truth to creep in. I was in love with Irene, and she with me. But somehow my deep sense of shame was still holding me captive. It was one thing to be rejected by other girls, but to find what I longed for only to remain in pain was an alarming twist. As I've come to learn intimately over my adult life, it is excruciatingly difficult to experience the love of another person truly if I cannot love myself. After a couple years I fell into an addiction to pornography, not realizing at the time that it was a way for me to obtain false intimacy without risking rejection.

I had graduated from college by this time and was attending seminary. The last thing I was prepared to face was people finding out my secret. I was completely unable to express any of my feelings. When Irene and I eventually began addressing our issues, I often had to write my thoughts and feelings out. Verbalizing them was too difficult. I was struggling immensely. I remember at church feeling like a complete phony as a visiting pastor spoke on the dangers and destructive power of pornography.

I was in so much pain. Fortunately I have gone through a lot of healing, so sometimes it's difficult for me to remember how bleak it was. I was completely lonely. I was full of shame. I was behaving in ways I never imagined I would. I felt God's disapproving eyes scowling at me more than ever. It seemed it didn't matter what I did. I was full of shame, whether I lived out my religious duties or I failed miserably.

Thankfully at that time a lifeline was thrown my way. Two of my sisters had recently participated in a spiritual formation seminar called Breakthrough and had found healing moments there. They had been talking to me about it often, so much so that I was becoming really annoyed. I didn't really want to look into it. It was expensive and sounded incredibly uncomfortable. I was growing increasingly desperate, though, so after months of dismissing the seminar, I finally looked into it, realizing that if I didn't do something, my situation would never get better. To my surprise my wife, who had also been annoyed by the persistent advertising, agreed to go as well. The night of the opening session we ate dinner at Panda Express, and expressed hope that this adventure would give us something we had been deeply missing.

The seminar was unnerving, but there was something welcoming about it too. It was sort of like seeing a doctor for an issue I hadn't wanted to face. I'll hate talking about it, but I'll also be relieved that it's finally going to be addressed.

Over the course of the seminar it was communicated to me that I was letting others control my life. In fact, I enjoyed allowing others to do so because it was familiar and easy. But if I was ready and had grown weary of living someone else's life, I would have to decide to change it. After being challenged to take the first step, and becoming very angry at the truth revealed, I rose up against the chains that had been holding me back. At that moment I felt a love I had never experienced and a strength I didn't know I had. I remember standing in the seminar room, roaring as loud as I could, like a lion that had been released from its cage.

It was a pivotal moment for me. I came face to face with myself and the way I had kept my heart locked away. Over the next few weeks I experienced life around me in a new way. It was like getting my ears unclogged and hearing sounds I forgot existed. I remember walking in the grocery store and having this unfamiliar sensation of being happy for no apparent reason. Somehow deep down it felt as if this was actually supposed to be my default mode.

As wonderful as this experience was, I soon faced a dilemma. The love I had experienced in that seminar was what I was longing for. It was everything I needed. The problem was it did not mix well with the religion I had grown up in and the gospel narrative I knew. Eventually I was going to have to choose one or the other.

I had just finished my second year of seminary. I was on track to graduate the next year, but I couldn't go back. The thought of pursuing that anymore felt lifeless. I couldn't bring myself to open the Bible, let alone teach it to others. I wanted to follow the love I had experienced, but leaving everything behind felt like leaving a significant other.

I finally broke down one night in the summer of 2008. I was delivering pizza at the time. On my way back to the store from a delivery, I made my choice. I told God that I couldn't handle trying to jump through the hoops to make him happy. No matter what I did my shame only grew stronger. I couldn't follow a temperamental taskmaster anymore. "If that's who you are," I concluded, "Then I'm done."

It was the hardest choice I have ever made. I was letting go of everything I had known. But something unexpected happened. I heard a voice, not audibly I don't think, but distinct. "That is not who I am." Instantly a sensation came over me, and I knew that the love I had experienced was

God all along, only I didn't recognize him. As Jacob expressed it, "Surely the Lord is in this place—and I did not know it!"[1]

The last ten years have been a journey of discovering who this love really is. The God I had ended up with back then was a volatile, almost schizophrenic being. At times he was forgiving and merciful; at other times he was bloodthirsty and harsh. Instead of running to him for comfort, I often did everything I could to keep him at bay. He was the monster in my closet, and I would do whatever I could to ensure that he remained there.

God had, however, revealed himself to me as a love deeper than I had ever known, and he was inviting me to rest in that security. The problem was that I had no training for that. My theology and my spiritual narrative revolved around a monster in my closet. If I was going to move forward, I would have to discover a new Gospel to live in.

1. Gen 28:16 (New Revised Standard Version).

CHAPTER 2

The Never-Ending Embrace

LAST CHAPTER I FILLED you in on the intense insecurity that has been a huge part of my life, but it's definitely not a problem that is unique to me. We don't have to scroll through social media for very long to see how central it is in people's lives. We often feel the need to remind ourselves of how special we are, and that we don't have to let others bring us down, because otherwise we will succumb to the pain.

I imagine that's why we are so easily offended. How upset should it really make us when another disagrees with our view on raising children, or with the political candidate we think is superior? We build our identities upon such fragility. We don't so much become offended as we become afraid, afraid that what we've built our lives on isn't really worth that much, and afraid of looking wrong to others.

Deep down, so many of us are just afraid that we are not enough or that we won't measure up. We feel we have nothing solid, nothing worthwhile within us, and so we seek to find it elsewhere. I've spent much of my life wasting energy consumed with this very dilemma.

I think that's part of what's going on in the story of Adam and Eve. Before everything falls apart, the story portrays them as having an intimate and meaningful relationship with God. Not only that, but they are perfectly free to be real and vulnerable with each other. "And the man and his wife were both naked, and were not ashamed."[1]

This intimacy with God and each other is what the serpent attacks as he twists God's words around to Eve. This is where the fall happens. The

---

1. Gen 2:25 (NRSV).

serpent convinces Eve that God does not want what's best for her, that he is withholding something good. When Eve believes the lie that God is holding out on her, she does what we all do: assume that something is wrong with us.

That's the dilemma so many of us face. How many times do we absorb someone's negative reaction into ourselves and assume it says something about us? I've often been reminded that if someone is short with me that it has more to do with them, but the very fact that we require that reminder shows how insecure we can be. We take so many cues from other people without even realizing it.

We seek validation and affirmation from others because deep down we doubt that we really have it from God. That's part of the consequence that Adam faces from the fall. "By the sweat of your brow will you have food to eat" is not a punishment from God, but the viewpoint of life one has when he assumes that God is absent.[2] It's all up to me if God has abandoned me. If I think that disownment is real, I will in turn assume it's because deep down I'm not enough.

There is something beautiful about the Christian faith, and what Christians claim to believe about Jesus, that could be the remedy for this dilemma, or at least ease our anxiety. The New Testament puts it a few different ways:

> "The Word became human and made his home among us."[3]

> "Christ is the visible image of the invisible God."[4]

> "The Son radiates God's own glory and expresses the very character of God."[5]

> "We proclaim to you the one who existed from the beginning, whom we have heard and seen. We saw him with our own eyes and touched him with our own hands. He is the Word of life. This one who is life itself was revealed to us, and we have seen him. And now we testify and proclaim to you that he is the one who is eternal life. He was with the Father, and then he was revealed to us."[6]

The early church affirmed this, but spelled it out more explicitly in the Nicene Creed, proclaiming that Jesus was "God from God, Light from Light, true God from true God; begotten, not made, of one Being with the

2. Gen 3:19 (New Living Translation).

3. John 1:14 (NLT).

4. Col 1:15 (NLT).

5. Heb 1:3 (NLT).

6. 1 John 1:1-3 (NLT).

Father." They also asserted that Jesus had become human "for us . . . and for our salvation."[7]

In short, we believe that somehow, in Jesus Christ, God has united with humanity. The technical expression is that Jesus Christ is God incarnate. Evangelical Christians claim to believe this. We celebrate it every year at Christmas. Honestly though, I don't think we take it seriously enough. At the very least, we don't comprehend the full implications of it, let alone allow it to impact our day-to-day lives. And the reason is this: we don't really believe Jesus became human. Instead we simply believe that he became *a* human. That is, we tend to believe he became a human being without uniting himself with all humanity.

When many evangelical Christians speak about the Gospel, they tell a story that sounds something like this: "God created us to have relationship with him. We chose to go our own way, and because God cannot look upon sin nor leave it unpunished, he sent his Son into the world to take the punishment as one of us. So if we accept what Jesus has done for us, we will be forgiven and go to heaven when we die. However, if we reject him in this life, we will face everlasting punishment after death."

That's the Gospel many Christians adhere to. It's the message I knew growing up and into my adult years. While I celebrated it then, I have many reservations about it now. It's not merely because I have an intellectual problem with this understanding; it's because it simply doesn't work as good news, and because it falls miles short of what Jesus really promised us.

In this story, Jesus simply has to become a human being. He had a specific mission to complete: die on the cross and rise from the dead. Curtis Freeman, putting it bluntly, writes, "The incarnation does no theological work in evangelical theology. It only serves the functional purpose of getting Jesus to earth so he can die for our sins."[8] His connection to us doesn't really matter. The only reason he is human is so that when he is punished, he is punished as a representative of humanity, which requires him to be one of us, but not necessarily one with us. In this story line, Jesus pays the price, and we simply choose to accept it or face the consequence.

It's sort of like this: one day I was in a drive-through to get an iced coffee (which I have a mild addiction to). When I pulled up to the first window to pay, the window was closed and no one was there to take my money. I was a little confused, but I didn't want to hold up the line, so I pulled up to the second window, assuming I would pay there. Instead, I discovered that the person ahead of me had paid for my coffee. Obviously I was excited about

---

7. "The Nicene Creed," lines 8-11, 13.

8. Freeman, "Faith of Jesus Christ," 6344.

the stranger's generosity, so I took my coffee and enjoyed the gift. A gift was provided, the price was paid, and I accepted that message.

Here's the thing: I didn't need to know that stranger to accept the gift. I didn't need to have any connection to her, or her me. In the same way, according to this version of the Gospel, we don't have to have any previous connection to Jesus in order to accept the price he's paid. This turns the Gospel around on its head, because instead of a relationship being established by God in the incarnation, it is instead established by us, by "asking Jesus into your heart," as the saying goes.

We have this beautiful and powerful movement in the incarnation. It's powerful because it redefines what we believe to be our position in reality. Yet we often don't really accept it for all that it is. Instead, we end up giving conflicting messages in the watered down gospel that we frequently tell. We proclaim that we are saved by grace alone, but with our next breath we also assert that only those who have faith, and by that faith ask Jesus to come into the center of their lives, will be saved. In other words, their faith is the act or work that saves them.

The incarnation, however, tells a much different story. It tells us that Jesus has already entered the center of our lives. It tells us that the deepest longing of our souls is already true. And it's true because Jesus became human, not just a human, and intimately united himself completely with all humanity.

I suppose we shouldn't be surprised that we try to make the Gospel about us. We tend to be pretty egocentric. This is our enduring problem. We don't trust that we already have what we're seeking, so we try to accomplish it ourselves. That's why, in our version of the Gospel, it is our faith, our response that culminates in the connection of Jesus "coming into my heart."

I believe this is partly why there is so much anxiety in our society, and particularly for those who would identify as Christians. I know it has been the case for me. This message sells the Gospel incredibly short. If it was my faith that made the cross effective in my life, if it was my prayer that finalized the connection between myself and Christ, then what about the days when I just don't feel it? What about the days when I genuinely doubt that God even exists, let alone that he died and rose again? What about the days when I just keep screwing up? If it was my prayer, my act of faith that got me "saved," then it depends upon me. And to be honest, there are some days that I'm just not very dependable.

The true Gospel tells us a much different story. It tells us that this whole process was initiated by a God who exists in relationship. The incarnation then becomes not just a rescue project, but an adoption process. Humanity is embraced in the life of God. You are embraced, and so am I.

The story is about participation in something bigger than us. Just as when a couple desires to have children, their own or adopted, they do so because they want to share the love flowing in their family. The affection and desire they have for each other is too dynamic, too large to keep between them. Their child then comes into a larger story; a story that has already been initiated and accomplished; a story which she is freely invited to participate in; a story for which she was created. Whether or not she chooses to live within the story doesn't negate that she has been chosen and embraced.

I can't overstate the importance of this perspective, or the impact it has had on my life. I grew up inside the false story. When I say that, I don't mean to insult those who taught it to me. It was what we knew. Within that context I gave my life to Christ when I was 6 years old, right around the time I began experiencing my dad's stress and interpreting it as abandonment. (Children simply cannot understand that such experiences are not about them, or that their parents are dealing with their own inner struggles). This molded me into a people pleasing, weight-of-the-world on his shoulders, deeply insecure little boy. I went to the altar of our church and asked Jesus into my heart, maybe because I believed it would fix everything. While it served a function for a time, eventually it only furthered my dilemma.

It furthered my dilemma because an added dynamic enters into this gospel narrative. We are told that it is our profession of faith that accomplishes the transaction. We are told to simply accept that Jesus has paid a price that we could not, and look forward to our eternal reward. But soon comes the catch: on our way there, we're supposed to act Christian, whatever that means.

Do you see the problem? Is it any wonder why so many Christians seem to be living a double life? It's because our gospel narrative requires behavior without giving any help. We're initially promised that we simply need to sign for the package that is being delivered by believing that a transaction was completed on our behalf. We later find out that an important piece was left out. Anxiety finds its fuel as our story begins without being embraced by Christ, and then proceeds with the requirement to be Christ-like. No wonder I felt I was having a nervous breakdown at times.

But I was a good little boy, wanting to make God and my parents happy, but ever wondering, does anyone really know me for who I am?

As I said, I can't overstate the impact this has had on me, though I've spent much of my life pretending everything was okay. That all changed for me as it so often does: I faced a crisis that my old way of living could not work through.

Five years into our marriage my wife and I were at a crossroads. We loved each other dearly but, as often happens, had hurt each other deeply. We didn't know how to communicate with each other. We were both living from our wounds; thus, every word and action was filtered through our brokenness.

There we were, not wanting to get divorced, but also not knowing how to make our marriage work. I had tried to work the system, play the religious game, and this was where it got me. We sat together on the counselor's couch. All my defense mechanisms were failing me. I remember expecting the counselor to offer some strategies and tips for better communication or something along those lines. Instead, she instructed me, "You need to realize how much God loves you." I didn't see that coming.

My life and my marriage were a complete wreck, and much of my part was because I didn't know this simple, yet life changing truth. I had developed a sense of abandonment, first by mistakenly believing that my father had rejected me when I screwed up, but ultimately from a God who I believed was never pleased with me. I had sought after any way to make the pain go away, and I believed that if I could just find that one special person to say "I do" and accept me unconditionally, then I would be free. But after 5 years of marriage, I had to face the truth: No person can ever do that for me. I was created to bask in Divine love.

The incarnation proclaims what we all need to know: we have been embraced, and God is never letting go. And this is in no way tied to how well we believe or how many good days we have. God, who exists in relationship as Father, Son, and Spirit, has decided to include us in that very relationship. He has done this simply because He loves to share. As Richard Rhor puts it, "God does not love you because you are good, God loves you because God is good."[9]

It really goes deeper than that, farther than we can imagine. We are told that, in the beginning, we were created in the very image of God, who is the Father, Son, and Holy Spirit. His intention was immensely deep and pivotal. Eugene Peterson puts it this way in his paraphrase of Ephesians:

> "Long before he laid down earth's foundations, he had us in mind, had settled on us as the focus of his love, to be made whole and holy by his love. Long, long ago he decided to adopt us into his family through Jesus Christ."[10]

God adopted us in Christ, but even that's really not the starting point. Going even deeper, somehow Christ has always been linked to the material creation, giving it life and direction, or as Colossians puts it, "Everything got started in him and finds its purpose in him."[11] In some mysterious and

9. Rhor, *Things Hidden*, 164.

10. Eph 1:4-5 (Message).

11. Col 1:16 (MSG).

moving way, the incarnation then is merely the logical conclusion of what was started in the beginning. It's as if by becoming human, God was simply giving more finality and intimacy to his original purpose.

This is God's plan, his intention, and it was his pleasure to accomplish it. He has "reconciled everything to himself."[12] Unless we capture that, we put the weight of it all on ourselves, we picture God to be angry and distant, and we start to lose our sanity. It's hard enough when another person has a vendetta against us, but so many of us view God this way and wonder why our heads and hearts hurt so much.

The Mirror Bible puts it succinctly:

> "To be persuaded about sonship as unveiled in the Son is to fully participate in the life of the ages! To be unpersuaded about sonship is to remain in blindfold mode to life itself in the here and now and to exchange fellowship with the Author of the life of our design for a fearful image of a vengeful, merciless god - quite the opposite of the loving Father the Son reveals!"[13]

The Gospel is about participating and celebrating in what is already true about Christ and, by extension, about us. It's incredible when we recognize what God has done, accept it, and join into it. If one wants to do that through a prayer, that's great. That's not, however, the beginning of the story; that's not where salvation starts. As Karl Barth responded when asked when he was saved, "It happened in a.d. 34, when Jesus was crucified and God raised him from the dead."[14]

Say the sinner's prayer if you like, but from God's perspective you don't need to ask Jesus into your heart; he's already there. Seeking forgiveness is still important, but from God's perspective you don't need to ask; it's already offered. Just like the Prodigal son, neither your worst days nor your most sincere moments of repentance change God's stance or attitude towards you. Your actions, your prayers, your prostrations will never be powerful enough for salvation.

If you've struggled with legalism, perfectionism, or people pleasing (like me), you probably have warning sirens going off in your head. "What about doing what's right? What about practicing the faith?" The reality I've found in my life and struggle is this: if I don't truly have the freedom not to do these practices, I won't have the energy to do them. They are meant to be sought after as if our soul's health depends on them, and that cannot happen when we are chained to religious bondage.

---

12. Col 1:20 (NLT).

13. John 3:35-6 (The Mirror).

14. Wood, "In Defense," para. 24.

A child can thrive, not when she believes her place in the family is dependent on her behavior, but when she knows her place in the family is never in question. When it is in question, all sorts of unhealthy emotional states and behaviors manifest themselves. The child develops a deep sense of insecurity. Anxiety can set in as well as a depression, stemming from the child's conclusion that something must be wrong with her. Destructive and unhealthy decisions follow and, if not addressed, can lead to a very dysfunctional life. Is this not the picture of so many people in our society, in our churches, and in our families?

This is what happens to humanity when it has a distorted image of God. This is why Adam and Eve hid and covered themselves up, and why we continue to do so. They believed a lie about God which in turn became a lie about themselves. They had messed up, and they feared that God would come after them. Of course, God did come after them, but not in the way that they anticipated. That's the point of the story: it is not we who go looking for God as if we have to convince him to love us. It is God who comes looking for us. We are the ones who have turned our backs. As Paul tells the Corinthians in the fifth chapter of his second letter, God has already reconciled himself to us, now we must be reconciled to him.

This resets how we imagine the Gospel and what Jesus accomplished. Jesus doesn't merely become our representative, but instead wraps humanity into himself. Jesus is humanity reconciled to God. What he does, then, is not simply done for us, but also as us, and to us. What Jesus does through the cross, resurrection, and ascension creates a shift in human reality. Paul indicates in several places that in Jesus something foundational has happened to humanity. As humanity was broken through our turning away, in Jesus, humanity was made right. Or as Peterson phrases it, "Everybody dies in Adam, everybody comes alive in Christ."[15] This is about realizing what has been made true. Through Christ we are restored, not by an impersonal transaction, but through fundamental transformation.

We need this rediscovery of the Gospel. Just like little children, we cannot thrive if we think the foundation of our relationship with our Father is separation and animosity. So many Christians cannot share their faith because it's simply not good news. They are burdened with anxiety and want to spare those around them the torment they themselves endure. But we do have good news to share, something that can truly set people free, something that has the power to break the chains of so much anxiety, depression, and spiritual dysfunction that runs rampant around us, among us, and within us. We do have good news: God is love. He has embraced us, and he's never letting go.

15. 1 Cor 15:22 (MSG).

CHAPTER 3

When God Can't Stand To Look At You

IF YOU ARE A woman in a significant relationship with a man, be it a boy-friend or a husband, may I give you a tip? I promise, it's a really good tip. It could save you hours and hours of heartache. It could keep you from wasting time trying to figure out why we think and act the way we do. Are you ready? Here it is: When it comes to relationships, men can be really dumb. Don't get me wrong; we totally have a ton of redeeming qualities that will make the journey worth it, but you just have to bear with us sometimes. So when you're wondering why we respond to relationship issues in bizarre ways and think, "Can they really be that stupid?" Why yes, yes we can.

When I was in college, we had to take a class on marriage and family. Our professor wanted to save us a lot of heartache, so he gave us as many tips as he could. One such tip concerned how important it is for people to express their feelings without someone evaluating them or trying to fix them. I got a heads up on this, and I still was very, very bad at the process. I've had to learn time and time again that sometimes Irene just needs to vent, and I just need to listen.

When Jesus was hanging on the cross, he understandably had to vent as well. He had to express how he was feeling. So he did when he cried out, "My God, my God, why have you forsaken me?"[1]

We have often assumed a particular message from Jesus's lament. We've ascertained that God truly did abandon Jesus on the cross, that he looked away. In church services we listen to sermons about this, as well as sing worship songs that proclaim this perspective. The reason behind the

---

1. Matt 27:46 (New International Version).

the courage to venture out toward God when we are essentially told that God can't stand to look at us?

This was a big reason why my marriage became so unhealthy, and why I was drowning in depression and anxiety. Nobody knew me, not even my wife, not even God as far as I was concerned. Sure, God knew me because he knew everything, but I wasn't going to address my crap with him. I wasn't going to risk the blowback from that. I also had too much shame and insecurity really to let my wife in. Eventually, it felt like we were roommates instead of husband and wife. If that was going to change, I would have to venture out to a God who saw the real me without cringing.

It's odd that we could get so convinced of God's inability to look at sin, or to be in the presence of sin, when this was the most common accusation that Jesus received. How many times in the Gospels do we see the Pharisees getting on Jesus's case about eating, welcoming, and associating with "sinners"?

The Pharisees didn't do this out of arrogance or hatred as much as from a religious agenda. The Pharisees looked around at what the Jewish people had endured over the centuries. Time and time again they had been conquered and forced to live amid foreign powers. It forced them to ask the question, "Why is God allowing this?"

They answered that question by using a time tested strategy: scapegoating. The chosen victims were sinners. Anyone who was violating the law of God qualified. Of course, the law invited, if not demanded, interpretation, so assigning the label "sinner" was a pretty subjective process. Regardless, the conviction was that sinners were the problem. In the Gospels, Jesus never seems to get with this program. He's always eating with the outcast, healing the untouchables, and breaking all the rules in order to bring the sinners back into the fold.

In spite of Jesus's example, we still fall back to our uglier tendencies. We see this in political, religious, and social circles. Why are we so quick to try this tactic over and over again?

Part of the answer can be seen in how often people are found to be projecting their own issues onto others. Think of the scenarios where a prominent religious leader rails against homosexuality or sexual promiscuity, and then is found to have a secret gay relationship or to be soliciting a prostitute. Victims of abuse often have their unresolved pain pour out on those around them. Thankfully, perhaps miraculously, there are also amazing cycle breakers. Unfortunately our scars and wounds often go unaddressed, or actively ignored, and end up manifesting in destructive behaviors. God's indication that sin will continue to affect a family for three or four generations seems to have some profound truth.

In short, the reason we so easily scapegoat others is that we so instinctively scapegoat ourselves. As we learn more about neuroscience and psychology, it becomes painfully evident how much suppressed pains and scars manifest themselves, but all our egos know how to do is condemn and hate. We don't want to feel sad, or broken, or weak, so we often punish ourselves for having those realities inside us. It feels easier to punish ourselves than to face our inner complexities.

We want our world to feel safe, to make sense, and to be predictable. When something gets in the way of that, all we know is how to condemn and cast out. We punish ourselves for constantly sabotaging our relationships. We ostracize people for asking the difficult questions and not getting with the program. We hate the little voice in ourselves that wants love, healing, and resolution. It'd just be so much easier if that voice would go away.

What we see in the life of Jesus, thankfully, is his unwillingness to cast away the people and issues we just want to avoid. Instead of avoiding the outcast lepers, Jesus heals them to bring them back within the community. Instead of disregarding the disturbed man roaming around the graveside, Jesus enters into his pain and brings healing.

Jesus does this on a deep, personal level; he won't let people just gloss over their inner pain. He cares too much to do that.

Think of the woman at the well that Jesus encounters in John chapter 4. She wants the quick fix that she hears Jesus talking about. She wants the never ending water supply. Jesus won't let her off that easy. He points out the pattern she has of going from one man to another, looking for someone to see the real her. She's so desperate that, most likely, she's now with a married man, perhaps hanging on his promise to leave his wife for her. She'd rather ignore this shady part of her life, but Jesus knows there is healing needed there before she can move forward.

There is also the woman who reached out in desperation for Jesus's cloak, believing that just a touch would bring an end to her constant bleeding. Her condition had made her an outcast in her religious community, so she's accepted that she's not worth the attention. She intends to just get in and out as quickly and discreetly as possible, but Jesus will have none of it. He calls for her, inviting her to have the courage to show herself, and then affirming her courage by claiming her as his own as he looks into her eyes and dotingly assures her, "Daughter, your faith has made you well."[3]

Or what about Peter? He had so confidently assured Jesus that here was one friend who would never forsake him. But in the throes of suffering, Peter denied even knowing Jesus. Now, following Jesus's gruesome death and resurrection, he and Peter are on the beach together. Jesus keeps asking

3. Mark 5:34 (NLT).

this difficult question: "Do you love me?" This is such a painful question. If you've ever failed someone, or betrayed someone, you know how hard it is to look at your shortcomings. Jesus is recorded as using the word *agape* for love, the most profound concept of sacrificial love that they had in the Greek language. Of course, Jesus likely wouldn't have spoken this conversation in Greek, but there's something important the author wants us to see. Jesus asks the question with the word *agape*, but Peter answers with the word *philo*, meaning a more informal brotherly kind of love. Peter is convinced that this is the best he can offer. Jesus keeps asking the question, and Peter keeps answering the same way, with Jesus responding, "Feed my lambs." Jesus is inviting Peter back into the fold, but it's only if they address Peter's deep wound: his failure as a disciple and a friend.[4]

I remember after I had shared with Irene about my time being addicted to pornography. I just wanted to bury it, never talk about it. Each time she brought it up, it was like a knife to my heart. I didn't want to look at my weaknesses. But she wasn't bringing it up to shame me, or to kick me while I was down. She wanted to find healing together. She wanted me to know that as much as it hurt, she forgave me. She wasn't kicking me down, she was inviting me back in. She was saying, "I believe we can do this."

So there is Jesus, asking Peter a third time, "Do you love me?" It's certainly no coincidence that Jesus does this three times, mirroring Peter's three betrayals. Seemingly to add insult to injury, Jesus uses Peter's word for love this third time. Peter is understandably hurt. He doubts his own ability to love and honor his friend, and now it appears that Jesus sees the failure that Peter sees. Instead, Jesus is going deep into the wound to offer a word of healing. He tells Peter, "When you are older, you will face pain and death, but through it you will glorify God."

Can you sense the relief that Peter must've felt? He doubted his ability to stay faithful to his friend; yet, Jesus tells him that he would bring glory to God. Jesus is saying, "I know you think you're a failure, but that's not what I see. I see something special, something strong. I believe in you."

We assert that God can't look at sin, but really it's we who have the inability to do so. We claim that God can't look at our darkness, but it's we who try to cover it up. We see our pain, failure, and shadow. We see hopelessness, but God sees the seeds of salvation. God goes into the darkness and beckons us to venture in with him. "If any want to become my followers, let them deny themselves and take up their cross and follow me."[5]

Often when we talk about taking up our cross, we focus on the sacrificial love that Jesus shows, and how we are invited to show that kind of love to others. That's a beautiful aspect of the Gospel, and I don't want to

4. John 21:15-19 (NIV).
5. Matt 16:24 (NRSV).

downplay that at all. But before we can truly get there, before we can combat the darkness in the world, we must face the darkness within ourselves.

It turns out there is a God in my closet, but he's not the menacing monster I had imagined. He's not there waiting to pounce. Instead, he's there embracing the skeletons I just want to ignore. He's embracing the wounds that have festered since childhood, the failures I've faced, and the rejections that have battered my heart. I'm the one who wants to ignore the darkness. God only knows how to love it.

The parable of the prodigal son illustrates this so profoundly. We assume that God is the one who cringes at our darkness, who becomes enraged at our failures and unattractive qualities, but in the parable it is the sons who are unable to handle their own dark sides. The younger son deals with it by beating himself up, and by offering to become a servant so he can ignore his own brokenness. He acknowledges his failures, but quickly comes up with a solution so he can brush past it. He offers to be his father's servant, because becoming a son is going to require a journey into the darkness.

The older son handles his brokenness by spewing anger out toward those around him. He casts his bitterness over his father and brother, and in all likelihood, he's been stewing in it for years. He's served day after day, not because he was offering himself freely, but because he expected something in return. Perhaps he wondered if there was something wrong with him, some reason why he didn't get what he wanted. Imagine the moment of clarity as his father says, "Son, you are always with me, and all that is mine is yours."[6] You could have had a party any day of the week, but you were too blinded by your pride and bitterness.

This is the tragic twist of our theology. We claim that God can't look at us because of our mistakes and failures. Such an idea only contributes to shame and fear, which contributes to depression and anxiety. These debilitating conditions make it virtually impossible to live the abundant and free life God has given us. We think we're solving the problem, but in the end, we only make it worse.

The truth is that God sees each one of us with the same doting love as a good father sees his son or daughter. He sees the truth of who we are. When we forget, he reaches out to remind us. I couldn't believe this for a long time. To be honest, there are still days where it is difficult. When I screw up, or am triggered by something around me, I have trouble seeing who I really am in Christ. But that struggle to see my value is mine, not God's. And it is that very struggle from which, and through which, God seeks to redeem us.

6. Luke 15:31 (NRSV).

CHAPTER 4

Separation Anxiety

HUMAN BEINGS LOVE STORIES. They have a power of giving meaning and inspiration to our lives. Little children love it when their parents recount a fantastic tale before they shut their eyes to sleep. We are gripped by stories of our families, our country's origin, or even background tales of how a local restaurant came to be. This has been the case throughout human history. Even going back several millennia, there are familiar themes that occur again and again.

One such theme is the loss of identity or home, and the ensuing journey that takes place to reclaim it. This can be seen in the ancient story of the Odyssey, as well as recent stories such as Cinderella or the Lion King. These types of stories speak to us because they ring true in our lives. It's the same for stories in scripture. We see a similar loss of identity in Genesis 3. We could argue that most, if not all, of scripture is the journey to recover identity, but with a deeper sense of who we are.

In Genesis, God creates Adam and Eve and invites them to partake of almost everything in the Garden of Eden, including the tree of life. This is quite significant, and in contrast to other creation stories in the ancient world. Often the tree of life is forbidden to humanity because the gods seek to keep a barrier between them and their mere mortal underlings. In Genesis, however, we already see the generosity and bountiful nature of Yahweh, as he invites Adam and Eve to partake in the same life he enjoys.

There is one item that is forbidden—the tree of the knowledge of good and evil. In this warning we see a window into the problem humanity faces. Most religion, at least the simplest form of religion, focuses on the knowledge of good and evil. Churches often focus on moral effort and knowing right from wrong. How ironic that this is what is forbidden in the garden. The inclination of humanity, which some would term "original sin," is to seek knowledge of good and evil. Yet churches often provide more of the problem (a hyper-focus on the knowledge of good and evil) thinking it is the solution—the very thing that God keeps from Adam and Eve. If they shared in the life of God (represented by the tree of life) everything else would fall into place.

On with the story. Along comes a serpent to wreck everything. He appears on the scene to tempt the happy couple with a poignant lie. He seeks to erode the very identity of the main characters. He begins with a subtle question: "Did God say, 'You shall not eat from any tree in the garden'?"[1]

The serpent begins by focusing on the one thing that Adam and Eve don't have. We so often equate sin with fancy temptations like illicit sex and money, but there's a deeper assault going on here. The serpent is trying to create a sense of incompleteness, to question the legitimacy of their personhood. So he starts by focusing on what they don't have.

How often do our down times start the same way? Why don't I have the happy family with three healthy kids? Why don't I have the prominent position where people admire and look up to me? Why couldn't I make my relationship work? So many of these questions stem from what we experienced as children and the resulting fear and shame.

What's wrong with me? Why am I so ashamed, or afraid, or angry? I would imagine most of us have asked questions like these, maybe on a daily basis, usually subconsciously. Maybe that's why we do so many things that we don't want to do, or why we have little understanding of our decisions. Maybe the guy in the gym every morning is desperately trying to feel strong; he feels small even when he's noticed. Maybe there's a woman working tirelessly to be chosen for a great position that deep down she doesn't even want; she needs to prove to herself that she's capable.

So the serpent begins with this deceiving question. Eve clarifies that it is only the one tree that is forbidden, and that death would be the result. The serpent then drops this bombshell, "You will not die . . . for God knows that when you eat of it your eyes will be opened, and you will be like God, knowing good and evil."[2]

Here's the thing: Adam and Eve already were like God. They were created in his image. The serpent puts the lie in the air that they are less than who God created them to be. He insists that God is for some reason withholding good from them. The message is simple: There's something wrong

---

1. Gen 3:1 (NRSV).
2. Gen 3:5 (NRSV).

with you, but I have a way to fix it. The way to fix it is eating from the forbidden tree to obtain by themselves what God had already granted them.

The story of the fall is about a loss of identity, the illusion that we are less than what God has created us to be, and what happens when we live out of that illusion. When we act out of that lie, there is a destructive force that works inside of us.

That's why it's so backward and damaging to talk about the Gospel as God having his mind changed in order to have a relationship with us. Much has been said about this view of the cross, and I'll get into it more later. At this point I'll just say this: We often talk about the cross as satisfying God's anger or placating his wrath, so the starting point becomes God's animosity and separateness from us. But God has never been separate from us; he has never disowned us. The fact that we think he ever has is the very problem of the fall; it is the basis of all sin.

Look how it plays out in Adam and Eve. They believe the lie that something is wrong with them, and that they are less than God's image. They then act out of this lie and eat the apple (representing a focus on moral effort) in an attempt to fix it. They lose their innocence; they lose their inner security, and they become filled with shame. When God shows up on the scene, they dig their hole deeper. They hide; they cover up; they are the ones who put up the barrier.

What does this story tell us? In reality, nothing that we don't already know. When we live in this lie, we experience shame. When we live in this lie, we cover up and hide. When we live in this lie, even the Garden of Eden can feel like hell. Living in this lie is the true meaning of sin.

The word for sin, *hamartia*, is often defined as missing the mark. In the context of dysfunctional religious environments and watered down gospel narratives, however, this is heard as missing the mark of moral conduct. Many believe that God's purpose is for us to be on our best behavior. Thus we have so many religious environments where people strive to follow the guidelines, but they are utterly miserable and full of shame on the inside.

Hamartia has less to do with behavior, and more to do with our identity, our God image. Francois du Toit, author of the Bible paraphrase *Mirror Bible*, writes that sin is to "believe a lie" about who we are, to lose sight of our "true identity."[3] When this happens, our lives become out of sync with who we are at our core: children created in the image of God.

We really need to reframe the issue we are facing. Sin is not primarily about our behaviors. Sin is a disorder (literally, our sense of identity is out

---

3. 1 John 2:1 (Mirror).

of order), a distortion in how we see reality. We need to get to the heart of the issue.

Imagine a young man, let's call him Dave, is dealing with weight gain. He just keeps eating and eating, and cannot seem to stop himself. He knows that it's bad for his health. He also knows that it keeps him from looking his best and from participating in physical activities. What he doesn't know, and is blind to, is that filling up on his favorite foods is the way he has learned to hide the shame and insecurity he feels. Telling him to stop eating isn't good enough because the root problem still exists.

So often in church circles we focus on the guilt of sin. There are times where guilt is appropriate and the process of forgiveness is needed. However, forgiveness only takes us so far. It is a means to the end: restored identity and relationships. Telling Dave that he should feel guilty for being so gluttonous doesn't really solve anything. In fact it can make it worse. Chances are he already does feel bad about it. The habit obviously needs to change, but if there is an unhealthy focus on his eating habits in the form of shame, it will only increase and amplify the problem.

The reality, however, is we must look at our sin, and the choices that we make. It's the only way we grow, and the only way we come to a deeper understanding of ourselves. Usually we either obsess about the ways we have screwed up, or we gloss over it and say, "I'm forgiven, so it doesn't matter."

I remember when I first began seeing my spiritual director. I was struggling with anxiety and depression, and I knew somehow that it had to do with my faith. A good spiritual director tends to speak the uncomfortable, often confusing, truths that we need to hear. That was true in my case. I was dumbfounded as my director talked about God leading us to look at our sin, and even that our sin is part of the salvation process. At the time I thought at best he was weird. At worst, he was teaching heresy. At the same time, something within me grabbed at what he was saying, like reaching for a branch while falling down a cliff.

The next time I saw him, I was still not too thrilled about the idea. To be honest, I had seen enough of my screw ups. For much of my life, faith mainly consisted of being reminded how I don't measure up. So as we sipped on our coffees, I informed him, "I don't think God wants to throw my sin in my face."

Good mentors have a way of picking up the nuance of the words we use. What he said in reply altered my journey. "No, God will not throw your sin in your face, because that implies condemnation. You have to understand that God is not out to get you; this is for your good. He intends to heal you, not condemn you. If you don't accept that about him, you will never move forward."

That hit home more deeply than I'd like to admit. The truth is I didn't really believe anyone was on my side. I've always been hypersensitive to critique because I have assumed that it comes from people seeing what I've thought about myself: I'm flawed, incomplete, and I don't belong. Those struggles come from not knowing who I am in the image of God, in Christ, and the results are the dysfunctional and destructive patterns I developed.

God leads us to look at our sin, which often starts by facing the symptoms of our sin. God led me to look at how I hurt people, how I live in fear, and how I find ways to fix myself instead of seeking him. My actions deserved to be called out, but that's not what God was doing. He was pulling back the layers to find resolution to what was really going on inside me. As Frederica Mathewes-Green puts it, "While our sins rightly deserve condemnation, God desires salvation, and his judgment is a blessing, the diagnosis that precedes healing."[4]

No one likes to be called out. No one likes to be told that his or her behavior is unhealthy and hurtful. We often don't even appreciate when our doctors tell us what's going wrong, even though we are paying them to do so. We get defensive when they critique our eating habits or our sedentary lifestyles. Sometimes we're exceptionally stubborn.

At times we're pitifully blind to what's transpiring on the inside. This began to become clear for me several years ago when my wife and I were taking a road trip to see family. We love road trips because it gives us a unique opportunity to be still together and talk. On this occasion, however, my wife was annoyingly observant. I don't remember what we were talking about, but at some point she chimed in, "You really don't like yourself, do you?"

I immediately became defensive; and yet, it was there for all to see except me. I beat myself up constantly. I was my own worst critic, and in a merciless and cruel manner. It was no wonder I was so depressed. The way I treated myself was atrocious. I would never stand for anyone else to be spoken to that way, but I had a different standard for myself.

So God took me down the road of looking at and bearing my sin with him. This was carrying my cross. It was painful, excruciating even, but it was for a deeper purpose. At the bottom of all my crap was a little boy who didn't believe he was worth loving. I had lost my identity; that was what my sin was all about. We focus on wild behavior or bad choices as the true meaning of our sin. They're just the symptoms. Our identity is lost. That's the core problem.

---

4. Green, *The Illumined Heart,* 49.

We begin to see, then, the backward nature of the gospel narrative told in much of our church culture. That narrative begins with a God whose attitude toward us is total animosity. He can't stand to look at us and will only do so once someone has been brutally punished. But this view of God is the source of our core problem. Adam and Eve hide from God because this is their distorted view of reality. As Richard Rhor points out, "You will never turn your will and your life over to any other kind of God except a loving and merciful one. Why would you?"[5]

The monster in my closet was God, or at least my understanding of God. Sure he gave his son to take the punishment for me, but if that's how he punishes his own son, how could I not live in fear? Once again, if my faith activates the salvation process, what about the days that my faith is not that secure?

This narrative begins with a God who rejects us and needs a transaction to accept us again, but if we are rejected, we lose our identities as children of God. To put it succinctly, the notion of being rejected by God is the essence of our sin, so to have a Gospel that begins with this premise is very problematic. If God can shift his fundamental attitude toward me, then I lose the foundation for my identity. So Jesus comes to show us how God really looks at us.

We still struggle with the notion that God's attitude toward us changes based on our behavior. But Jesus speaks of a Heavenly Father who treats everyone with the same grace, even those who consider him their enemy. "He causes his sun to rise on the evil and the good, and sends rain on the righteous and the unrighteous."[6] While the ancient world so often wondered what the gods were up to, why they blessed one day and cursed the next, Paul assured the Romans that God is for us. Therefore, nothing "will be able to separate us from the love of Christ."[7] This is not true about just a select few people, or simply those who are "in." If the incarnation is to be taken seriously, then this must be true for everyone. This is the Gospel hope that we are given. As Wayne Jacobson so beautifully puts it, "Jesus's purpose was not to make us worthy of God's love, but to set us free to see that we already have it."[8]

The famous philosopher, Plato, once gave an illustration of what it looks like to be set free. In his lesson, Plato likened our experience of reality to people being chained inside of a cave. There is a fire behind them,

5. Rhor, *Breathing Under Water*, 26.

6. Matt 5:45 (NIV).

7. Rom 8:39 (NRSV).

8. Jacobson, *Finding Church*, 1117.

and they are confined in such a way that they cannot turn their heads to see it. As activity takes place behind them, but in front of the fire, shadows are projected onto the wall of the cave that the prisoners are facing. Thus the shadows are their entire concept of what reality is. It is only by being unchained that they can ascertain what is really happening.

Plato then hypothesizes that if one of the prisoners were to be set loose from his chains, and allowed to exit the cave into the real world, the experience would be incredibly jarring and painful. He would have become attached to the shadows, even giving them names and titles, but now he would face the startling discovery that it was all a facade. It would be an uncomfortable shift physically as well. His eyes would have to adjust from years of near darkness to explosions of light and color. It would be a difficult adjustment, but his experience of life would unquestionably be superior to his time in the cave.[9]

The notion that we are separated from God is our fundamental problem. It is not reality; instead, it is simply a shadow on the wall. We try to fix the separation with our religious efforts and moral strivings, but there is nothing outside of us that needs to be fixed. It is our perception that needs adjustment, just like the prisoner's perception in the cave. Jesus reveals to us what is really going on: We are embraced, and God is never letting go.

This is the reality that God wants us to live in, but we have to go through the darkness to get there. We must see how we buy into the lie, and are paralyzed by the fear in our hearts. We fear people finding out about our deepest darkest secrets, and so we run away. We avoid, we deceive, and we manipulate all to hide our shadows.

I lived this way much of my life. It was my way of surviving. In reality it was actually killing me. I needed to be able to open up to others by learning to accept myself, but I could only do this if I truly believed God loved me and would never leave me. To move in that direction I would have to find new ways of understanding the central aspects of my faith that have hindered my spirituality so much. That is what we turn to next.

9. Plato, "Book VII," 324-359.

PART II

THE BOOK BEHIND THE CURTAIN

CHAPTER 5

The Worst Instruction Manual Ever Written

THE STORY GOES THAT a warrior had been cast away from his family. He was the son of a prostitute, and for this he was driven away and given no part of his family's inheritance. He settled in another town. When his native people were attacked by another country, however, they came to the warrior and asked that he lead them. As you can imagine, he was very suspicious of their sudden positive disposition toward him. After careful consideration, however, he decided to be their leader.

The warrior set out against his enemy and was advancing forcefully against them. In the heat of battle he offered a vow to his God. He vowed that if he were given victory over his enemy and returned home, whatever emerged out of his house to greet him on his arrival he would sacrifice. When he came back home, his joy of victory quickly converted to grief as it was his daughter that greeted him first. Though deeply saddened, his daughter agreed to the sacrifice, wanting her father to stay true to his vow.

This story is heart wrenching and tragic. If you are very familiar with the Old Testament, you may have recognized it as a story from the book of Judges, and recalled the warrior, Jephthah, as being one of those Judges who led part of Israel during that time. This story is heart wrenching. If you ever viewed the Bible the way I grew up understanding it, it also raises some very difficult questions.

As an Evangelical, I was taught to view the Bible as God's word, or as being inspired by God. What that means exactly differs somewhat for different branches. Some view the Bible as having absolutely no mistakes in it: historical, scientific, or otherwise. This is often referred to as an inerrant view of scripture. Others view the Bible as being faithful and trustworthy in all things related to salvation. This is sometimes termed the plenary view of scripture. In my experience, many Evangelicals who belong to a denomination that asserts the latter (plenary) will, for all practical purposes, engage the Bible with the former (inerrant) view. Whether Christians view scripture as inerrant or not, most tend at least to view the Bible as being faithful in its portrayal of what God is like. At times we have what some term a "flat view" of scripture, meaning that whether we are reading from Joshua 10, Judges 10, or Matthew 10, whatever picture of God is offered is equally inspired and equally revelatory of his character.

When we read a story like the one I just recounted, however, these views of scripture become troubling and lead to some difficult questions. For example, in this story we are told that the Spirit of the Lord was on Jephthah as he went to battle. Does this mean that God favors violence? Does it mean that the same Spirit of God was the one who directed Jephthah to offer his vow? Does this story mean that God values child sacrifice? And how can that be when in other places God specifically denounces child sacrifice as evil?

In short, if the entire Bible faithfully portrays the character of God, then God has some very questionable behaviors. Before we offer up the "God can do whatever he wants because he's God" argument, let's at least acknowledge that if a world leader were to carry out or command some of the acts that are attributed to God in the Bible, most of the world would demand that leader be arrested, if not executed, for his war crimes. From commanding genocide to sacrificing the firstborn of an entire nation, God is often involved in some very horrifying situations.

Yet these are mixed with some polar opposite accounts of God's involvement. God is often portrayed as incredibly compassionate, especially toward the poor and oppressed. While he sometimes comes off as a hothead, other times he has incredible patience with the stubborn, pain-in-the-ass people he is trying to lead. So which is it? Does God have an affinity for violence and retribution? Or is he "slow to anger and abounding in steadfast love"?[1] Or perhaps he has multiple personalities.

Or maybe, the problem is with us and the way we understand the Bible. Either way, I needed a resolution. I had come to believe that God truly was love. I believed my encounter with him was genuine and it changed my life. For a while, however, I was not able to approach scripture. It was volatile and toxic for me. While I was following the freedom God was offering me, I seemed to be pulled back into dysfunction and unhealthy spirituality whenever I attempted to engage scripture. I had to give it up for a while, and

---

1. Ps 103:8 (NRSV).

it has been refreshing to discover this to be a common theme in the spiritual journey of many others.

Evangelicals value the Bible very highly. We descend from the Protestant tradition that views the Bible as our ultimate authority. The scope of authority that scripture has is, however, understood differently. Some view the Bible as authoritative on everything, such as a scientific account of the origins of the universe. Others don't view its authority quite as expansively. Most Evangelicals, however, at least view it as authoritative for our moral decisions and in revealing God's character.

When I was a teenager, our youth group was given a book that had Bible verses listed by topic to answer all of life's questions. Whether we were wondering about abortion, God's view of sexuality, or how to pray, we could turn to a chapter of this book and find all the verses associated with that topic. The Bible was essentially viewed as our instruction manual for all of life.

We take for granted that the Bible was always understood this way and always viewed as our ultimate authority. As Phyllis Tickle demonstrates in her book *The Great Emergence*, however, there appears to be a five hundred year cycle when our religious culture is forced to face the question, "Where now is our authority?"[2]

Roughly one thousand years prior to the reformation, the authority was the creeds of the church. As tensions grew between the Eastern and Western realms of Christianity, this authority was questioned. The Great Schism then took place, with the authority shifting, at least in the west, over to the Pope. This was where authority for the western church stood for centuries and, obviously, still does for the Catholic Church. Eventually, however, a dilemma arose as three different men were roaming around Europe each claiming to be the rightful pope. The accepted authority was eroding, and the search for a new source again began in the reformation.

As most of us know, the new authority became scripture. This became increasingly possible as the printing press made the Bible more readily available. Eventually, rather than spiritual authority going through a single person, individuals would have access to the Bible to read and interpret for themselves. This was not the overnight result, of course, but it was the direction in which we turned.

We have benefited from this tradition, as well as inherited some unexpected consequences. We are experiencing a time of growing pains and experiencing new worlds. The reformers were questioning their old authority in the papacy, or at least the way the authority was used. In the same way,

2. Tickle, *The Great Emergence*, 777.

we are now being forced to ask some crucial questions about the authority of scripture, or at least the way we understand the scope of that authority and how we approach it. These are not trivial or simply rebellious questions, either. They are crucial because of what we have seen and experienced. As Rob Bell is so fond of saying, "Once you see, you can't unsee."[3]

So, for example, we view scripture as our authority and as the source of what we are to believe. If that is true, then, which translation of scripture are we going to engage? There are many different translations, and even when composed by a plethora of authors, the translations tend to reflect certain theological biases. In fact, many passages in scripture do not allow a straight translation. In order for it to make sense, the translators have to insert their interpretive bent.

More fundamental than translations, however, is which canon we are going to use. The collection of sixty-six books many hold to be the inerrant word of God is not even the agreed upon canon for the universal church. In reality, no such canon exists, because while we hold dear to our collection of books, the Catholic canon has books that we Protestants do not include. The Orthodox Church has more still. The idea that the Bible is our ultimate authority becomes somewhat suspect when, though these canons are vastly similar, there is no complete agreement on what our Bible should contain, let alone how it should be interpreted.

Protestants, and evangelicals in particular, pride themselves on their love of scripture. After all, one of the developments of the reformation was that the sermon became the centerpiece of the worship service. It is ironic then that the Protestants, who asserted that our foundation should be "scripture alone," would proceed to remove books of the Bible that had been in the Catholic canon for a thousand years. In addition to this, Martin Luther wanted to remove James, Jude, Hebrews, and Revelation from the canon as well. It becomes convenient to assert that the Bible is our authority when we are able to craft the structure of it in the first place. I don't say this to pick on Martin Luther and others, but simply to point out what happens with all of us. Our view of the Bible is formed by our particular theological and interpretive lens, and it would be better for us to acknowledge this rather than pretending that the Bible, as our authority, can somehow be interpreted objectively.

Translations and canons are two issues concerning the authority of the Bible. Another development that has led to many questions is our interaction with social issues, particularly over the last 150 years. Many Christians have believed the Bible to speak uniformly on the pivotal issues of our lives.

3. Bell, *What Is the Bible*, 3.

I recall being told while growing up in the church and attending Christian college that there are no contradictions in scripture. If they appear to be present, it is because we misunderstand the text. This assertion has come under great scrutiny.

One pivotal social issue, which we are learning still exists among us, is slavery. When we look back over our history, it is almost unfathomable to think that slavery was an accepted reality for much of that time. In America, slavery is an uncomfortable reality of our past. For hundreds of years it was central to the economy of the "new world," (new to Europeans, that is) and was an accepted institution. Over time an understanding of the inherent value of all human beings began to erode the foundations of this evil.

The acceptance of slavery is astonishing to us now. What is equally, if not more astonishing is the fact that many Christians were using the Bible to justify and preserve it. The assertion was that because slavery was accepted in scripture as lawful, we must accept it as well, even if we have a moral aversion to it. Essentially, if the Bible includes it, we better get on board with it regardless of how we feel.

On the one hand, this assertion is correct. There is no place in the Bible that explicitly says slavery is wrong or immoral. While there are passages in scripture that insist on love and compassion toward our fellow humans, there are also other passages that insist on faithful service of slaves to their masters. The bottom line is that if we approach scripture as an instruction manual, we have typically come to the conclusion that slavery is an accepted reality.

Many Christians, however, could not go along with this. They asserted, as we do today, that though slavery was seen as acceptable in those times, we cannot now allow it to continue if we are to take the life and teachings of Jesus seriously. That is to say, the Gospel offers us a path and a view of reality that will increasingly open us up to new understandings of what justice and righteousness look like over time. The authors of the Bible, because of their limited time wrestling with the Gospel and being caught up in the customs and realities of their culture, could not see the absolute immorality of slavery, or at least could not see the possibility of ending it.

Another social issue we have faced is women's rights, especially concerning divorce. The church had often taught that women should keep silent, even as their husbands were beating them. Over time the voices of battered women and children were taken more seriously. Where once divorced men and women were treated as outcasts, they are now allowed ordination within many denominations. It is clearly a step in the right direction to encourage women to leave abusive husbands. It does leave us wondering, however, how to interpret passages in scripture that once seemed so black and white.

In addition to these social issues, many Christians view the Bible vastly different because of advances we've had in science. We now have a very different understanding of how the natural world works, how societies work, and how our minds work.

We also have a much greater understanding of what the ancient world was like, as well as access to other writings in the ancient Middle East. We know now that many ancient civilizations had their own flood stories. We also know they had creation myths, and we can recognize the similarities and connections between said stories and the accounts in Genesis.

All of these factors make it virtually impossible for us to view the Bible the same way. Is the Bible inspired? I believe it is, but what does that really mean?

The common verse for talking about the inspiration of scripture from 2 Timothy reads, "All Scripture is inspired by God and is useful for teaching, for reproof, for correction, and for training in righteousness."[4] This doesn't settle things as neatly as we would like. Depending on the date attributed to the book of 2 Timothy, it was written many years before the church began to settle on a New Testament canon, and most likely even before other books of the New Testament were written. In all actuality, therefore, this statement about the inspiration of scripture could only have been referencing the Old Testament scriptures at the time. It leaves us asking the question, what does it mean for the Bible to be inspired? We don't want to come away with an assertion that the Bible doesn't even make about itself.

Frankly, I'm ready to be done with trying to prove the Bible is what we think it is. So much time has been spent either memorizing scripture to have the most knowledge, or trying to prove how the Bible is historically accurate and therefore reliable. Lots of books are historically accurate. That's not necessarily the best criteria for settling the inspiration argument. Furthermore, if we can prove that the timetables and geographical references in the Bible are accurate, how does that make us more loving and compassionate people? Shouldn't that be the goal, to be more like Jesus?

This is why how we view the Bible is important. I, like many Evangelicals, was advised that if I want to be a better Christian (to worry less, to love more, and to experience peace), then I should read the Bible more. Read it every day. That's exactly what I did. I would read, and read, and read. I memorized scripture for Bible quizzing. There were a lot of benefits to this,

---

4. 2 Tim 3:16 (NRSV).

of course, but over time the Bible, due to my understanding of its authority, became less helpful in my faith quest. Frankly, it became disturbing at times and downright toxic, because of how we tended to use it.

Of course, scripture, and any truth for that matter, is meant to be somewhat unsettling, especially if we are not lined up with it. But how was I supposed to line myself up with a God who taught to love our enemies, but often decimated his? How was I supposed to conform to a God who supposedly teaches that we experience tough times because of sin, but who also taught that "blessed are those who are persecuted"?[5] Most troubling, how was I supposed to warm up to a God who sent his Son to save me, but would also punish me severely for all eternity if I didn't have proper belief in his son? These conflicting images were anxiety inducing.

This is the dilemma: imagine getting hired for a great position. You begin your first day excited to learn and improve your skills. You were pleased by the demeanor of your manager during the interview, and today you are to meet with him briefly to prepare for the day.

"Are you nervous about your first day?" he inquires.

"A little. You know, I want to do a good job and all."

"I'm sure you do. I want to assure you that we are a team here, and we don't let people fall through the cracks. So if you're having a tough time with any part of the job, please feel free to ask questions and know that we will always be willing to help."

You leave your brief meeting with the manager feeling excited to get started, and supported in your new position. Partway through your shift, however, you start to notice that some of the employees don't seem quite as thrilled as you are. In fact, some of them appear to be downright miserable. So while on one of your breaks, you decide to make a comment just to get a feel for what your co-workers are thinking.

"I really like our manager; he's very supportive and helpful," you remark.

"Yes he's great," one of your fellow workers responds, "but make sure you steer clear of the owner; that guy's not someone you want to mess with."

"Really? Why's that?"

"That guy will kick you to the curb just for looking the wrong way."

How would you feel working in an environment like this? I can tell you how I felt. I worked in a technology position where the workers and the lead were incredibly helpful, but the boss was domineering and harsh. If you asked a genuine question, you would be looked at as stupid and not

5. Matt 5:10 (NIV).

worth the time to answer it. It was chaotic and dysfunctional. After a month I nearly had a nervous breakdown.

The way we typically view scripture left me in a similar environment. I needed a better notion of inspiration. Saying it is the word of God doesn't really help me. Claiming that there are no contradictions is simply dismissive. I needed to begin my notion of inspiration where I begin every other part of my faith: at the feet of Jesus Christ.

CHAPTER 6

Reading with Jesus-Colored Glasses

I IMAGINE MOST OF us have experienced it. Maybe we're walking in the city, or stopped at an intersection, and we look over to see that familiar eccentric character holding a sign. The screaming or dancing grabs our attention. We look over and see that old time sentiment that often makes our eyes tumble backwards: Repent! Repent of what, I'm often not sure, but apparently something is off that needs to change. Most often the motivation behind the sign is that God is coming back soon, and he's apparently not very happy. God is pissed, and he's about to lose it on us. When this is our view of God, our faith becomes one long attempt to keep on his good side.

I had a custodian position back when I was in college. It was a great gig. Whenever I finished my work early, I would get a lot of my studying done. I worked the evening shift. On my first day of work, the boss called me in his office to explain the dynamic of our relationship. Because he ended his shift at 2:30, and I began mine at 3:00, I would usually never see him, unless I was in trouble. "Your goal in this job should be to never see me," he reinforced. "If you have to see me, it means something is wrong."

That was how I viewed God for much of my life. I would do everything I thought I needed to do—go to all the church services and events, pray, read my Bible—so that I wouldn't get on God's bad side. God was the ogre in charge that I wanted to avoid, and all my efforts kept any shame and brokenness at a distance.

Then one day I encountered divine love, but in my quest to work past the monster that had grown up in my mind, I was facing a serious dilemma: the Bible kept tripping me up. There were some amazing passages in scripture that were mind blowing. I had been so blinded by my fear, however, that I had missed some powerfully freeing messages. I was still facing my dilemma, though. As beautiful as God appeared in some passages, he appeared equally ghastly in others. The Bible was supposed to be a source of spiritual growth for me; instead, it had become a source of spiritual poison. God appeared, at best, to be two-faced and unstable. I could not warm up to a deity like that.

On the other hand, however, Jesus was someone whom I could trust. So many vulnerable people in his day, who would've found it impossible to open up to anyone else, seemed to sense something safe and secure about him. He offered rest, peace, and mercy. While there were some passages in the Gospels I was uncomfortable with, I somehow knew that I could trust him to lead me in the right direction.

Jesus could be very firm and confrontational at times. He was not afraid to call people out, and could use seemingly harsh words in the process. A religious leader using those tactics would often be a huge turnoff to the people outside looking in. People outside the religious circle (and many inside of it) don't want to hear about repentance. This is the very sentiment that Jesus began his ministry with; but somehow, the prostitutes, the outcasts, and the moral failures felt completely comfortable around him. Somehow, so did I.

One reason was that Jesus's harshest words were reserved, not for the "sinners" or the rebellious, but for the religious elite. He called them out, often accusing them of using their religious influence to make others miserable and treat them like dirt. They were upset when a deformed person was healed because it violated their religious norms. They designated other people's sinful behavior as the reason for the national failures, but wouldn't do anything to help them. As Jesus put it, "You shut the door of the kingdom of heaven in people's faces. You yourselves do not enter, nor will you let those enter who are trying to."[1] Jesus's life was defined by compassion, so he chastised anyone who used a religious guise to treat someone poorly. Thus the sinners, the children, and the outcast were drawn to him.

These conflicting portraits of God were distressing. Most of the time when I read scripture, I was suffering from a sort of religious post-traumatic stress disorder. I was seeking the God of love; but inevitably, I would run into a wall. As good Evangelicals, we were taught that all of the Bible was inspired and faithfully conveyed the character of God. But when that lens is taken off, for whatever reason, we're faced with something so obvious we're a little embarrassed we didn't see it sooner. There are some blatant contradictions in the image of God we are given in scripture that can leave us feeling as though we're dealing with multiple personalities.

---

1. Matt 23:13 (NIV).

In my quest, I was asking for a decent explanation for the issues I was seeing. Unfortunately in religious circles, even at the college level, people are often uncomfortable discussing such issues. How could Jesus teach love of enemies and bottomless forgiveness when his father seemed to go on violent rampages at times? How could God's mercy be described as "never ending" when he was destined to punish eternally those who were not loyal to him? How could I warm up to a loving father whose sole basis for accepting me was his redirected anger and retribution on Jesus? I was seeking the God who had recently revealed himself to me as love incarnate, but I was having difficulty moving in his direction.

It was about this time that a mentor directed me to a significant point that Jesus makes in the Gospel of Matthew. I had grown up in the church, had read the Bible several times, and was two years into a seminary degree; yet, somehow I had completely missed this passage. "My Father has entrusted everything to me. No one truly knows the Son except the Father, and no one truly knows the Father except the Son and those to whom the Son chooses to reveal him."[2]

This was one of those paradigm, earth shifting moments in my life. The Bible was supposed to have been infallibly conveying the character and will of God; and yet, Jesus seems to say that before his arrival on earth, this wouldn't have been possible. He seems to be saying that Moses, David, Joshua and scores of other heroes of our faith did not truly and completely know God, at least not to the intimate extent that Jesus did. This sent tremors through my understanding of faith.

What did this look like? One very intriguing example is the story of Elijah from 2 Kings. The story goes that the new King of Israel, Ahaziah, had fallen and badly injured himself. He wanted to know what his outcome would be, but instead of consulting the God of Israel, he sent his messengers to consult the foreign god Baal-Zebub. Because of his unfaithfulness, God told Elijah to intercept those men and inform them that the king would die.

After running into Elijah and receiving his message, the men returned to the king to tell him the message from Elijah. The King, obviously not happy with the message, sent fifty soldiers and their captain to find Elijah and bring him back. The captain called out to him, "Man of God, the king has commanded you to come down with us."

Elijah, without flinching, replied to the captain, "If I am a man of God, let fire come down from heaven and destroy you and your fifty men." Then fire fell from heaven and killed them all."[3]

2. Matt 11:27 (NLT).

3. 2 Kgs 1:9-10 (NLT).

Elijah proceeded to do this to the next group that the king sent. When a third group approached, the captain begged for mercy, and Elijah agreed to go with them.

Now let's fast forward several hundred years to Luke chapter 9. Jesus and his disciples decide to journey to Jerusalem as it is approaching the end of his ministry and the time of his crucifixion and resurrection. To get to Jerusalem they need to go through Samaria, where citizens despised Jews and Jerusalem. Because of this, some Samaritan villagers refuse to accept Jesus and his disciples into their town. The disciples, upset at how Jesus was treated, offer to punish them and ask Jesus, "Do you want us to command fire to come down from heaven and consume them?"[4]

Now if you're like me, you might be wondering why Jesus would call such psychopaths who would seek to destroy anyone who disagreed with them to be his disciples. To the disciples, however, this would be following in the footsteps of one of their faith heroes. Elijah did it, so it would only make sense for Jesus and his disciples to act in the same way.

Jesus disapproved of their request. Some manuscripts even have Jesus elaborating by saying, "You do not know what spirit you are of, for the Son of Man has not come to destroy the lives of human beings but to save them."[5]

Jesus strongly disapproves of such behavior, and in doing so calls into question the actions of Elijah, especially if he did clarify "You do not know what spirit you are of." If that's the case, what spirit was Elijah following when he acted in this way?

The question here is essentially this: Does Jesus endorse the entire breadth of what is communicated in the Old Testament, particularly what is communicated about God's character? In my experience the answer among Evangelicals is usually a resounding yes, but why is that? How do we come to this conclusion? Michael Hardin offers a possibility and critique when he writes, "Protestants frequently argue that because Jesus quoted the Jewish Bible, this means that he accepted its authority as a whole. When they do this they import a modern view of the authority of Scripture back into the past."[6]

We often assume that the Jews of the first century had an agreed upon view of scripture and its authority, but in Jesus's day there was no such consensus. Some groups viewed the Torah, the historical books, and the prophets as having different levels of authority. It's noteworthy that Jesus himself never quotes scripture from any of the historical books.

4. Luke 9:54 (NRSV).
5. Luke 9:56 (NRSV).
6. Hardin, *Jesus Driven Life*, 1488.

Jesus does tell us that he comes to fulfill the law and the prophets, not to abolish them. But as Derek Flood points out, "This is often taken to mean that Jesus is in complete agreement with the law, ignoring the rather obvious fact that the very next thing Jesus does after saying this is to proceed to blatantly contradict and overturn multiple Old Testament passages and principles in the rest of his sermon."[7] Jesus clearly doesn't view and apply scripture the way we tend to.

Protestants view the Bible as the ultimate authority. We assume that first century Jews, including Jesus, viewed the Hebrew Scriptures this way too. In a new shift, however, many New Testament writers see in Jesus the inauguration of a new starting point. Jesus more than hints at this in a rebuke to his Jewish accusers, "You search the scriptures because you think that in them you have eternal life; and it is they that testify on my behalf."[8]

What Jesus said was incredibly astonishing, as well as controversial. He was putting the scriptures in a different category. They were not the end, but a means to the end. Jesus essentially puts himself above them, and offers himself as the true revelation of God.

He does this in the Sermon on the Mount as well. "You have heard that it was said . . . But I say to you."[9] It's interesting that He does not say, "God said," or even "Moses said." He is communicating that no one really knows the Father except him, that he reveals the Father in a unique way.

The early church confirms this in their writings:

> "The Word became flesh and lived among us, and we have seen his glory, the glory as of a father's only son, full of grace and truth."[10]

> "He is the image of the invisible God."[11]

> "This life was revealed, and we have seen it and testify to it, and declare to you the eternal life that was with the Father and was revealed to us."[12]

The author of Hebrews spells it out even more explicitly:

> "Long ago God spoke to our ancestors in many and various ways by the prophets, but in these last days he has spoken to

7. Flood, *Disarming Scripture*, 32.
8. John 5:39 (NRSV).
9. Matt 5:21-2 (NRSV).
10. John 1:14 (NRSV).
11. Col 1:15 (NRSV).
12. 1 John 1:2 (NRSV).

us by a Son . . . he is the reflection of God's glory and the exact imprint of God's very being."[13]

The writer is essentially telling us that God spoke through his people in the past, but there was something incomplete, something missing. God is willing to descend to our level even if it means he's misunderstood at times. Now, in Jesus, we have the real deal. Now we can look at him and truly see who God is and what he is like.

There's an important point to see here. Jesus is revealing to us what God really looks like, but this isn't an Old Testament versus New Testament dichotomy. Though the Old Testament often looks barbaric and irrelevant to us, there are some truly remarkable trends going on through those pages. God, in speaking to his people, is working in an incarnational way. As Peter Enns explains, the Bible "belonged in the ancient worlds that produced it. It was not an abstract, otherworldly book dropped out of heaven. It was connected to and therefore spoke to those ancient cultures."[14] He is meeting people where they are and working through their culture, their worldview, and their personal experiences to communicate a message. Sometimes that message comes out clear, sometimes it's a little muddled, and sometimes it seems nonexistent. Even in those nonexistent moments, we see not only how people missed the point, but how we often do as well.

There are two streams or "trajectories" flowing through the Hebrew Scriptures.[15] Often there is sacrificial language and a focus on ceremonial perfection. Violent commands and acts are scattered throughout. God appears to be bloodthirsty and retributive.

On the other hand, there are moments of incredible compassion and mercy. There are times where God seems not only permissive of questions and bargaining, but actually welcomes them. God is said to command a certain way of living and honoring him, but as the story unfolds, God seems to contradict things that were previously commanded. At one point God, speaking through Hosea, tells his people, "I desire mercy, not sacrifice, and acknowledgment of God rather than burnt offerings."[16]

This just so happens to be the Old Testament passage that Jesus quotes most frequently. There's a message being sent through this. When Jesus comes along and says, "Do not think that I have come to abolish the law or the prophets; I have come not to abolish but to fulfill,"[17] he's not endors-

13. Heb 1:1-3 (NRSV).

14. Enns, *Inspiration*, 5.

15. Hardin, *Jesus Driven Life*, 4306.

16. Hos 6:6 (NIV).

17. Matt 5:17 (NRSV).

ing every portrait of God offered in the Hebrew scriptures, but instead is coming down on the side of mercy. There is a development going on in the Old Testament, and Jesus is showing us where the process points: "Whoever has seen me has seen the Father."[18] The early church truly believed this and viewed the Old Testament through the lens of Jesus. Compassion, love, and mercy were seen as the true revelation of God as opposed to violence, anger, and hate.

In the end Jesus still calls us to repent, but not in the way we often think. Sometimes we think of repentance as feeling sorry for something we've done. This reaction to doing something harmful or destructive is a natural and healthy response. In fact, we rightfully worry about someone who can act this way and have no remorse. But that's not what repentance is.

Sometimes we think of repentance as making up for the things we've done. There are times when this is helpful as well, and even necessary to experience healing. That's not repentance either.

Repentance is changing our minds, or having new insight into the way we operate that leads to a new direction. Repentance can be difficult. It involves difficult truths, but it is not mean, or harsh, or condemning. Sadly I viewed God this way for much of my life. I thought I needed to repent in order to avoid the monster in my closet. In reality, it was this very view of God from which I needed to repent. God is love; his mercy never ends. If I was going to have a faith that actually worked to address my depression and anxiety, this was the truth I needed to seek. This was the insight I was desperate for. Each day I must repent from believing in the monster.

So instead of looking at the Bible piece by piece as if it is all equally representative of God's character, Jesus invites us to look at him as the measuring stick. After all, Jesus prepared his disciples for his absence by promising that the Holy Spirit would speak to us all that Jesus wants us to hear, not a set of books. Jesus is our guide, our authority, and our measuring stick; turning to him can help resolve these troubling elements in scripture.

18. John 14:9 (NRSV).

CHAPTER 7

Walking On Eggshells

WHEN I WAS 6 years old my family packed up a moving truck and relocated to a new town in East Iowa. My dad had been interviewing to be the new pastor of a church in this new town. I had been kept in the dark, however. As a little boy with no filter, anything told to me could, and probably would, be blurted out at the most inopportune times.

Adjusting to a new town and school brought its usual challenges, but one situation made the process particularly difficult. A first grade boy in our class stood a head taller than the rest of us. He had a bad temper, and unfortunately he would often take it out on me. I was very shy and non-confrontational, so eventually I tried to get on his good side. You know the drill—tip toe around him, laugh at his jokes, and act like I liked him. In reality, however, he was the last person I wanted to be around because I never knew when he was going to blow up.

How similar this was to my fragile relationship with God. Sometimes I wasn't necessarily thrilled about him; I just knew what he was capable of. As long as his wrath wasn't directed at me, I would jump through the hoops set out for me. I could even be okay with his wrath being poured on others, as long as I was on the right side.

It was similar for some Jewish sects of Jesus's day. They had been conquered by empire, after empire, after empire, and they were waiting for the day God would rescue them. A prominent passage for this hope came from the prophet Isaiah. Michael Hardin cleverly points out the prominence of this passage: "Have you ever seen a football game where after a touchdown somebody holds up a sign in the end zone seats that reads "John 3:16?" If they had played football in Jesus's day that sign would have read "Isaiah 61:1-2."[1] These two verses proclaim,

> "The spirit of the Lord God is upon me, because the Lord has anointed me; he has sent me to bring good news to the oppressed, to bind up the brokenhearted, to proclaim liberty to the captives, and release to the prisoners; to proclaim the year of the Lord's favor, and the day of vengeance of our God; to comfort all who mourn."[2]

Central to the Jewish hope was that God would free them from the bondage they had endured. They knew intimately what it meant to be oppressed and captives to a foreign power, and they waited expectantly for their rescue. Their hope included another theme, however, and that was "the day of vengeance." In their minds liberation would not be complete without wrath being poured out over their enemies.

So when Jesus speaks in the synagogue in Luke 4, there is a reason that the people get so angry at him. Here's what we're told:

> "Jesus unrolled the scroll and found the place where it was written: "The Spirit of the Lord is upon me, because he has anointed me to bring good news to the poor. He has sent me to proclaim release to the captives and recovery of sight to the blind, to let the oppressed go free, to proclaim the year of the Lord's favor."[3]

Notice what Jesus does there. He reads this prominent and pivotal passage, but he stops short of reading about God's vengeance. He takes a vital part of their liberation vision and deliberately removes it. Imagine if a local sports team invited a prominent singer to perform the national anthem, and as she beautifully belts out the lyrics, she ends it prematurely and leaves out the words "and the home of the brave." You can imagine how offended and outraged the audience would be. The anti-military connotations would be obvious.[4] The connotations from Jesus's omission would have been obvious as well: God is not interested in vengeance, or retribution. God is not who you think he is.[5]

1. Hardin, *Jesus Driven Life*, 1535.
2. Isa 61:1-2 (NRSV).
3. Luke 4:17-19 (NRSV).
4. Zhand, *Sinners in the Hands*, 40-41.
5. Concerning the fact that most translations indicate that those present at Jesus's reading spoke well of him, Michael Hardin writes, "The Greek text is quite simple and the King James has adequately translated this "and all bore witness to him." This bearing witness in the KJV is neither positive nor negative. Why then do translators say, "all spoke well of him?" Translators have to make what is known as a syntactical decision,

If there was any doubt of what Jesus was conveying, he proceeded to remind the people of two occasions when a prophet of Israel was sent to serve a foreigner rather than an Israelite. Elijah, during a famine, was sent to feed a widow in Sidon, and his successor, Elisha, healed a Syrian. Again, Jesus's message is clear: God is not interested in vengeance or excluding Israel's enemies. Rather, he intends to fulfill his original mission—to be a blessing to the entire world. Jesus is challenging the way they operate, and the villagers respond by trying to kill him.

Through much of the Old Testament, God is seen as the rescuer of the Israelites, and almost by consequence, the destroyer of everyone else who does not get in line. We see this in one of the most gruesome missions God is said to command.

Saul has been chosen by God to be king, after God consents to Israel's desire to have a ruler. Samuel, the prophet who has led Israel, and through whom Saul was made king, gives Saul a task to accomplish:

> "This is what the Lord Almighty says: 'I will punish the Amale-kites for what they did to Israel when they waylaid them as they came up from Egypt. Now go, attack the Amalekites and totally destroy all that belongs to them. Do not spare them; put to death men and women, children and infants, cattle and sheep, camels and donkeys.'"[6]

If this passage disturbs you, you are not alone. Growing up I just read the Bible and simply took it at face value. I often didn't think of the implications, maybe because I didn't want to. We often look back at some of the atrocities throughout history, like the holocaust or the slaying of the Native Americans, and we wonder how humanity could have resorted to such barbarism. Yet here is God commanding the same level of horror—woman and children to be ripped from their homes and run through with swords or spears.

Why does God command such a thing? What had the Amalekites done that caused such vengeance? The offense of the Amalekites appears in

---

they have to decide whether or not the "bearing witness" is negative or positive. Technically speaking they have to decide if the dative pronoun "to him" is a dative of disadvantage or a dative of advantage; was the crowd bearing witness to his advantage or to his disadvantage? If it is the former case then the intonation we gave to "Isn't this Joseph's son?" above would make sense and Jesus immediately following gets sarcastic for no reason, but if it is the latter then we could just as well translate this text as "and all spoke ill of his sermon", that is, they didn't like what he said. Then the intonation of the phrase "Isn't this Joseph's son?" should be rendered something like "who does Jesus think he is coming into our synagogue and saying such things?" With this alternate, preferable translation, of verse 23 Jesus is not being sarcastic but is responding to the negativity of the listeners." (*Jesus Driven Life*, 1552)

6. 1 Sam 15:2-3 (NIV).

Exodus chapter 17 when they attack the Israelites as they journey through the wilderness. This is the story of a battle being won because Moses held up his staff in his arms. Whenever his arms were up, Joshua and the Israelites prevailed. Because of the attack, God vows to blot out the name of Amalek, and Moses declares that God will be at war with their descendants from generation to generation.

By the time Saul is given the command to wipe them out, it is hundreds of years later. That means we are dealing with people who had nothing to do with the attack. Also, God commands Saul to wipe them out, including women and children, which goes beyond God's own initial instruction to take an eye for an eye. This is escalation on a grand scale. Ultimately Saul wipes all of them out, but fails to kill all of the animals, which offends God enough to remove him as king.

What are we to make of this? Again, we could make the "God can do whatever he wants" argument, but is that really the character that Jesus reveals of his Father? Are we to view the Bible as "flat" with all its passages being equally authoritative, or are we to give more credence to the revelation of God in Christ? That's what the New Testament writers seemed to do, as well as the early church. Many Christians today often fail to follow their example.

The violence commanded by God against the Amalekites is by no means an isolated event, of course. There are the millions we are told who are killed in the book of Joshua during the conquest. There are the thousands of parents mourning the loss of their firstborn in Egypt. If we were judging all of this by our human standards we could understand. We've shown what we're capable of, and it's not pretty. But how do we line this up with the teaching that we should love our enemies so "that you may be children of your Father in heaven"?[7]

Or there is the incident in Numbers chapter 25. The Hebrews have been wandering through the wilderness after their miraculous escape from Egypt. While they are staying in a town along the way, however, some of the men start sleeping with the locals and engaging in idolatry with their gods. This stirs up God's anger, and he orders the leaders of his people to be killed. In the middle of this an Israelite man brazenly brings a local woman into his tent in front of everyone. Phinehas, the grandson of Aaron, has enough and takes a spear and runs the couple through together. God praises Phinehas and his actions, saying "he was as zealous for my honor among them as I am,"[8] the implication being that God's zeal is all about pouring out retribu-

---

7. Matt 5:45 (NIV).
8. Num 25:11 (NIV).

tion on those who anger him. Zeal, as it does for some groups within the Judaism of Jesus's day, becomes equated with violence. In many passages throughout the Old Testament, God is portrayed as a violent deity who is passionately opposed to anyone who stands against his people.

We see this played out in a prominent character of the New Testament. Paul was a man after Phinehas's own heart when we first encounter him in Acts. He stands approvingly by as the Sanhedrin members hurl their stones at Stephen. By Paul's own testimony he has shown his zeal by persecuting the church. He confesses to Timothy, "I was once a blasphemer and a persecutor and a violent man, I was shown mercy because I acted in ignorance and unbelief."[9] Paul was transformed, however, when he encountered the God who allowed himself to be killed rather than kill others.

This transformed the way Paul viewed his scriptures. He saw them differently, just as Jesus had. As Derek Flood demonstrates in his book, *Disarming Scripture*, Paul takes passages from the Old Testament that explicitly endorse violence against Gentiles and, by omitting the violent aspects, turns them into declarations of mercy. By removing phrases like, "I destroyed my foes . . . he is the God who avenges me, who puts the Gentiles under me . . . he will take vengeance on his enemies," Paul is redefining his image of God because of his encounter with Jesus.[10]

Jesus, Paul, and others in the New Testament are giving us different lenses through which to read scripture, and thus, through which to know God. Otherwise, we are left with a Bible that leaves us confused and handcuffed. Otherwise, we are left to wrestle with having a Jesus who tells us to love our enemies, who includes the outsiders, and who offers forgiveness to those who persecute him, and having a God who is a moment away from wiping everyone out, who holds grudges for centuries, and who makes children suffer for the sins of their ancestors.

How are we supposed to warm up to a God like that? As I mentioned before, I struggled for a long time to truly face my brokenness and screwups. The reason was that I never knew what kind of God I was facing. If I was dealing with Jesus, I could trust that he was working on my behalf. He might get blunt with me. He might tell me some things I don't really want to hear, but I could trust that he was on my side. Ultimately he was trying to teach me how to rest in his love. If, on the other hand, I was dealing with the God prone to violence and losing his temper, there was no telling what I was up against. He might take me through incredible pain simply to assuage his anger. After a while, I wasn't sure if I could take another bout of that.

9. 1 Tim 1:13 (NIV).

10. Flood, *Disarming Scripture*, 60-69.

The God that we often infer from these stories is an anxiety-producing God. We know what we are capable of. Even on our best days we fall short of our ideal. If God pours out destruction and vengeance on people who fail, how can that not fill us with crippling fear? If God's idea of righteousness is people being run through, like the couple killed by Phinehas, what will happen to us when we fall short?

Jesus offers us a different image of God. Imagine what Jesus would have done had he seen a couple committing adultery. Although, I suppose we don't have to imagine very much. After all, one half of an adulterous couple was brought before Jesus by the religious leaders in John chapter 8:

> "Teacher," they said to Jesus, "this woman was caught in the act of adultery. The law of Moses says to stone her. What do you say?" They were trying to trap him into saying something they could use against him, but Jesus stooped down and wrote in the dust with his finger. They kept demanding an answer, so he stood up again and said, "All right, but let the one who has never sinned throw the first stone!" Then he stooped down again and wrote in the dust.
>
> When the accusers heard this, they slipped away one by one, beginning with the oldest, until only Jesus was left in the middle of the crowd with the woman. Then Jesus stood up again and said to the woman, "Where are your accusers? Didn't even one of them condemn you?"
>
> "No, Lord," she said.
>
> And Jesus said, "Neither do I. Go and sin no more."[11]

The expectation of the accusers, as well as the woman, I would imagine, was for Jesus to seek justice via punishment.

With this image of God as violent and retributive, people often end up like either side in this story. If we are in touch with our frailties, it leads to the anxiety of the woman, anticipating brutal punishment and condemnation from those around her. On the other hand, those who cover over their shadow often project their own anger and self-loathing onto others, spotting every speck of dust they can. We end up in the "us versus them" game. This is what religion often reverts to.

This condemnation is not the power or force that transforms lives, though we continue to think it is. "Do not judge" continues to be an immensely challenging command. We claim not to want to be judged ourselves, but we instinctively rake others over the coals for the most minor offenses. Road rage is exceedingly common, even as it is obviously an utterly

11. John 8:4-11 (NLT).

ridiculous concept. Becoming enraged at such trivial things should have ended after childhood. Instead, our elementary behaviors carry over.

The reason we can't stop judging and condemning others is that we do the same to ourselves. We don't want to deal with the weaknesses and fears inside us, but we know they exist. We don't want to understand why we get so angry or are so prone to manipulate others, but it's clear that we do. We think it would be easier if it all just went away. So we cast it out. If anyone irritates us or brings out the dirt swept underneath our rugs, we'll cast them out too. We can't let them mess up our system.

For me to move forward, I needed that system to fall. In order for that to happen, I had to begin giving up my bipolar notion of who God is. I thought God was the bully, but in reality it was my own inner voice that was tearing me down. I made it my job to do. I had come to believe that a central aspect of Christian faith was judging things that were wrong. By judging we usually meant casting out, shunning, or dismissing that which made us uncomfortable. So that's what I did with the pain and sin within me. I condemned it, and in doing so brought condemnation on myself.

In Jesus's Sermon on the Mount he made a very curious, if not confusing statement. "But I tell you, do not resist an evil person."[12] It doesn't make sense to us initially. We think the way forward is through opposing, judging, and ridiculing. That usually gives evil more power. It fights force with force.

Let me give you an example. Athletes in the spotlight sometimes make very foolish decisions. It's not surprising. They are caught up in the spotlight with more attention and money than they've ever experienced. That is a dangerous mix for anyone, let alone barely adult (mostly) men who can be very immature.

Because they are in the limelight, their stupid mistakes get more attention. When one of their missteps is known or suspected, like taking steroids or behaving poorly on social media, they will inevitably be confronted about it. What's interesting is that the ones who own up to it are able to move forward more easily, and the media almost never brings it up again. But when they deny, become defensive, and snap back at their accusers, it's almost all the media can discuss. The fighting and resisting makes it far worse than it could be.

This happens on an individual level as well. When someone pushes aside or hides his problems like alcoholism, manipulation, or jealousy, it only makes the problems worse. We like to ignore our problems, but our blindness only fuels the situation. That is why, as the saying goes, the first step is to acknowledge that we have a problem.

12. Matt 5:39 (NIV).

We don't do this very well, and our refusal to accept and sit with what is going on inside us creates a host of additional problems within. Richard Rhor enlightens us:

"How long it takes each of us to just accept—to accept what is, to accept ourselves, others, the past, our own mistakes, and the imperfection and idiosyncrasies of almost everything. It reveals our basic resistance to life, a terrible contraction at our core or, as Henri Nouwen, a Catholic priest and writer, told me personally once, "our endless capacity for self loathing."[13]

No wonder we end up with so much inner tension. This is one of the reasons why discussing the apparent violence of God in scripture is pivotal. If we worship a God who is inherently violent and condemning, we will treat the dark parts of ourselves in a violent and condemning manner as well. We'll do this either to follow in his footsteps or to avoid facing him with such glaring deficiencies.

We need a God who is consistently good. We need the kind of Abba Jesus spoke of so fondly. The good news is that if we look closer in scripture, we will see that there is something different going on than we often imagine.

13. Rhor, *Breathing Under Water*, 18.

CHAPTER 8

He Will Beat Your Scriptures into Plowshares

"WHAT ARE YOU so afraid of?" My wife asked. We were seeing a marriage counselor as our relationship was struggling. We didn't really know each other, partly because I was afraid to open up. I would tense up anytime I needed to share something deep. There was some force blocking my ability to open up to her.

"I'm afraid of being rejected."

My wife chuckled a little, the kind of chuckle you give when you're completely confounded. "But I married you!" She exclaimed. "How can you be afraid of rejection?"

I didn't really understand it at the time either. In hindsight I can see how my habit of assuming everything was my fault led me to keeping Irene at a distance. I didn't want her to see what I believed to be true about myself—that I was no good. I feared that she would reject the real me, and I played it safe by not opening up at all. It didn't yield the results that I had hoped for.

Christians often take a "play it safe" approach to God. We refuse to look deep inside for fear of how God will respond to us. Much of this stems from our view of God that we infer from scripture. On the surface, many stories and passages in scripture seem to offer up a God who is very angry, judgmental, and retributive. There are other passages, of course, that offer a more loving and compassionate view. If used as our primary lens, they could bring insight to the former types of passages. And if we read the Bible with the context in mind, and through the lens of Jesus, we find that some of those seemingly harsh passages are perhaps offering a very different perspective. However, we sometimes take what we believe to be a less risky approach. We decide that if we live as if God is angry and retributive and, in the end, find out he is actually loving, then we have not risked very much. If we instead live our lives by living as if God is love and compassionate and come to find out that he really is the angry ogre we dread, then we will have risked much. This "play it safe" method doesn't seem to be the way Jesus viewed his Abba.

We often think we're playing it safe by approaching the Bible in a literal, inerrant, instruction manual kind of way. As I've expressed earlier, the Bible itself doesn't allow us to do this. The Bible doesn't claim this about itself, and there are too many tensions in scripture to use it as a flat-line piece of literature where every passage carries the same amount of weight. I've also pointed out that our lack of uniformity in canons and translations makes it impossible to use the Bible in this way. Most importantly, however, Jesus doesn't allow us to do this either, because no one knows the Father as he does.

Evangelicals often have the fear that if we don't get our biblical interpretation and theology nearly perfect, there will be dire consequences, even though we know that such precision is impossible. It also misses the element of wrestling with scripture and truth, much like Jacob wrestled with God. It might leave us limping, but we'll be better for the experience.

We approach scripture literally thinking it is the safer option, but it leaves us missing the point, because often it leaves us overlooking the genre we are reading. Rob Bell explains it well: "I've heard people say that they read it literally. As if that's the best way to understand the Bible. It's not. We read it literately. We read it according to the kind of literature that it is. That's how you honor it. That's how you respect it. That's how you learn from it. That's how you enjoy it."[1]

A better approach to scripture is one that takes the literary genre into account. Imagine 500 years from now someone getting their hands on the *Harry Potter* books. Perhaps they would be unaware of J.K. Rowling and her reasons for writing those books. What if, after reading through the series, two people start arguing about whether or not witches and wizards existed at the time the books were written? They may debate and throw pieces of evidence around, but wouldn't it be sad if, after all this time spent discussing the books, they would completely miss the themes of friendship, courage, and the importance of standing for what's right?

We need to read scripture by its genre, understanding that the culture and worldview of the times would have inherently impacted the message. We cannot expect the writers to talk in twenty-first century terms. When we do, we miss the point and make God to be in our own image.

1. Bell, *What Is the Bible*, 79-80.

The Bible, as Rob Bell likes to say, was written by "real people living in real places at real times."[2] God moves in an incarnational way and meets people where they are, but also tries to move them forward. Sometimes they get it, sometimes they don't, but there's a movement. Let's look at the movement in the area of violence.

History, the saying goes, is told by the victorious. The people who win battles and conquer other tribes can tell the story however they want. In ancient times, people had their tribal gods. When tribes fought each other, it was assumed that whoever was victorious won because their god was stronger. The defeated and victims did not have a voice. The gods were with the powerful.

That begins to change in the book of Genesis. We are told of two brothers, Cain and Abel, who both offer a sacrifice up to God. God accepted Abel's sacrifice, but rejected Cain's. Why? The only reason that is indicated is that something was not right in Cain's heart, and God tried to direct him in the right way. Unfortunately Cain gave into his anger and murdered his brother.

Then something astounding happens. Rather than siding with the powerful, God approaches Cain and informs him, "Your brother's blood cries out to me from the ground."[3]

There were similar stories among ancient peoples, but there's a difference brewing in this telling. As Michael Hardin explains, in the former stories, "The brother or sibling who dies got what was coming to him. Not so in the Genesis story, where for the first time the victim has a voice, it cries out from the ground for vengeance. Not only does God hear it but Cain is afraid others will hear it too and avenge the murder of Abel."[4]

This is God siding with the victim, but also refusing to continue the cycle of violence. God is seeking to nip the problem in the bud. God even puts a mark on Cain that prevents people from doing to him what he did to Abel.

A similar anxiety would have been present when Jesus appeared after the resurrection. The disciples, for the most part, had abandoned him during his crucifixion. Peter explicitly denied even knowing him three times. They were all locked up in a room together. Their leader had been crucified. Who knows what could happen to them? In comes Jesus, the friend they betrayed. Yet there's no vengeance or bitterness in his voice. Instead his first words are, "Peace be with you."[5]

---

2. Ibid, 21.

3. Gen 4:10 (NIV).

4. Hardin, *Jesus Driven Life*, 4744.

5. John 20:19 (NIV).

Jesus suffered greatly, but he refused to continue the cycle of retaliation. God sees us when we suffer too. He hears our cry. But we usually cry for vengeance; we want people to pay when they harm us. The next time we screw up, though, are we still going to seek that retributive brand of justice? Most people want retribution until they're the ones who need mercy.

Throughout history, even to this day, people, tribes, and societies seek out a scapegoat on which to project all their anger, shame, and conflict. The victims of this process never had a voice, never had anyone to stand up for them, to speak truth to the situation. In scripture we have a God who refuses to play that game, and stands up for those who are beaten down.

There are so many passages and stories that we have made to be about a violent God that, when read with the lens of Jesus and as literature, tell a different story. When we pull a retributive God out of these stories, we are making God in our own image, much like many of the biblical authors did because "no one truly knows the Father" like Jesus does. We project our anger, our shame, our bitterness, and our violence onto God. In a way, we make God out to be the patsy for the shady, hurtful, and evil things we do, and at times he lets us, because he does not use power to dominate or coerce.

This comes out profoundly in the story of the flood. When we read the flood story as a scene by scene take on history, we come away with more evidence that God is a hothead who supports violence as a means to make the world better. When read this way, however, we miss the elements in this story that subvert our normal tendencies. Many ancient peoples had flood stories; it was their way of explaining what they experienced around them. These stories also attributed the disaster to the gods, who had various reasons for wanting to wipe out humanity. The gods were often thought to be just as cranky, violent, and petty as we are, just bigger and stronger.

In the biblical account of the flood, however, God gives a reason for taking this action, and it's different than we often think. "The Lord saw how great the wickedness of the human race had become on the earth, and that every inclination of the thoughts of the human heart was only evil all the time."[6] We read that and tend to assume it is speaking of certain types of wickedness that might get emphasized in religious circles. We might think of drugs, or maybe wild sexual lifestyles. The story only mentions one sin specifically: "Now the earth was corrupt in God's sight and was full of violence."[7] It seems odd that a story often used to support violence actually begins with God speaking out against it.

6. Gen 6:5 (NIV).
7. Gen 6:11 (NIV).

Perhaps, then, this story is about God being in a position to use violence in the right way. This is how Christians often use this story. Sometimes it seems helpful to have a cosmic bogeyman to keep people in line. At the end of the flood, however, something unexpected takes place. God seems to regret what he has done, "Never again will I curse the ground because of humans."[8] Apparently violence never solves the problem, even when God uses it.

God does not operate as we do, and we see it come through beautifully in many stories. Take the story of Joseph, a favored son who can be a little much sometimes, but who is a beautiful soul who loves and adores his family. The preferential treatment he receives draws out the envy and inferiority complexes of his brothers. In their anger they turn Joseph into a scapegoat and sell him into slavery. Once again, God looks out for the victim, elevating Joseph in status and vindicating him to his family.

Joseph's slavery takes him to Egypt. Initially he is bought by one of the Pharaoh's officials. He is wrongfully accused of attempted rape, however, and is thrown in prison. Once again God looks after the victim and provides Joseph a way to gain Pharaoh's favor. He is looked upon with such approval that Pharaoh makes him his second in command.

This assignment leads to an opportunity for revenge. A famine hits the area, and Joseph's brothers are forced to travel to Egypt for food from none other than Joseph himself. Many people would be jumping at this perfect chance to get even. Instead, Joseph welcomes them with open arms. Later he tells them, "Do not be afraid! Am I in the place of God? Even though you intended to do harm to me, God intended it for good."[9]

Or what about the Exodus? Here are slaves oppressed by a super power, completely without a voice or any way out. But then, "The Israelites groaned in their slavery and cried out, and their cry for help because of their slavery went up to God. God heard their groaning and he remembered his covenant with Abraham, with Isaac and with Jacob. So God looked on the Israelites and was concerned about them."[10] God again stands up for the victim, the oppressed, and calls Moses to speak truth to power. God fights for his people and saves them. Is there violence attributed to God? Yes, but as Rob Bell points out time and again, "That's what people did at that time."[11] Yes, there are primitive aspects, but there are history altering aspects as well, like a God who stands up for slaves.

8. Gen 8:21 (NIV).

9. Gen 50:19-20 (NRSV).

10. Exod 2:23-25 (NIV).

11. Bell, *What Is the Bible*, 122.

Ultimately we get to Jesus, who proclaims a new kind of kingdom. He teaches about showing love and compassion, even for the people who stir up hate in us. Even one of his disciples feels the need to correct him. For most Jews the Messiah would violently and victoriously kick out their enemies. So for Peter, it was simply wrong to exclude this from the mission. Jesus rebuked Peter, saying, "Get behind me, Satan!"[12] The Satan is the accuser, seeking to create "us versus them" dynamics. This wasn't what Jesus was after.

Even Jesus's cousin, John the Baptist, had his doubts at one point. In Luke 7 John sent two of his disciples to Jesus to ask if he really was the one they were waiting for. Jesus responds by referencing the miracles he has performed, but in doing so, he is also referencing passages from the prophet Isaiah. What's the significance? "The Isaiah texts all include a reference to the vengeance of God none of which Jesus quotes."[13]

As he did in Luke 4, Jesus is reframing what it looks like to be like God, and what it looks like to live in his kingdom. Many believe that John was part of the Essenes, who anticipated the apocalyptic overthrow of those they believed were impure. John may have been trying to make sense of a Messiah who was not seeking the same thing.

Not only did this fly in the face of many Jews at the time, but the Roman Empire as well. Many of the keywords and phrases used by Jesus and the early church challenged the imperial way of life around them. The phrase "Caesar is Lord" was co-opted to confess Jesus as Lord of a very different kingdom, one where rulers conquer through sacrificial love. The Greek word for Gospel, *euangelion*, was originally connected with the news of Roman military victory. The church instead used it to speak of a different way to triumph.

Jesus becomes the scapegoat, the victim, rather than victimizing others. We can see that Jesus's accusers believe that if they can just get rid of him, everything will go back to normal. Jesus allows it, asserting that he could call angels to step in, but he is showing a better way. He follows this way all the way to death. He refuses to seek retribution, and instead he seeks forgiveness for his executioners.

Jesus refuses to act violently or seek retribution against his enemies. This all seems to change, however, in the book of Revelation. John, the author of Revelation, uses violent imagery throughout. Thus, many Christians assume that Jesus, one day outlined in the future, will return in vengeance

12. Matt 16:23 (NIV).

13. Hardin, *Jesus Driven Life*, 1610.

with a ferocity that will make Rambo look like a teddy bear. A few notes, therefore, need to be made about this book.

Revelation has had a complicated history within the church. "It's the book that had the hardest time gaining admission into the New Testament canon of Scripture."[14] It was not accepted as canonical by the Eastern Church until several centuries later. Martin Luther barely wanted to include it in the protestant canon. One of the reasons is that the Christ interpreted out of Revelation often looks like an anti-Christ.

Some of these interpretations have come out in popular books and movies depicting end times and the apocalypse at the hands of a violent, warrior Christ. Armageddon takes place and the world comes to an end. Such a view mistakes the book for a timeline of the end of the world. This gets several pivotal points wrong.

Firstly, the book of Revelation is not mainly focused on the end, rather it is seeking to encourage those suffering at the hands of imperial oppression to stay the course. Ted Grimsrud echoes this when he writes, "The biblical use of apocalyptic language, like the broader use of prophetic and eschatological language, serves the exhortation to faithfulness in present life."[15]

Secondly, Revelation is not portraying a God who ultimately wants to destroy the earth, but one who wants to save us from our own destructive ways. Once again, it is our self-condemning ways that are the problem. And once again, we project them onto God. Armageddon literally means "valley of Megiddo." This is an area in the Middle East that, because of its strategic location, was coveted and fought over time and again. Thus as Brian Zhand puts it, "Armageddon isn't the end of war; Armageddon is endless war."[16] Jesus seeks to save us from such destructive patterns.

Lastly Revelation does not campaign for a violent Jesus, but instead uses powerful imagery to remind us of Jesus's victory through self-giving love. This comes out most powerfully in the fifth chapter. A scroll is revealed to John, but it seems there is no one able to open it up. Just then, John is assured that "the Lion of the tribe of Judah, the Root of David, has conquered, so that he can open the scroll."[17]

Judah was the father of one of the twelve tribes of Israel, and Jesus was a descendant. This is a reference to Jesus, and lion is a symbol of power and might. The notion that power and might are what produce victory is not surprising, but what happens next is. John looks and sees "between the

14. Zhand, *Sinners in the Hands*, 148.

15. Grimsrud, "Biblical Apocalyptic," 4.

16. Zhand, *Sinners in the Hands*, 170.

17. Rev 5:5 (NRSV).

throne and the four living creatures and among the elders a Lamb standing as if it had been slaughtered."[18] This is pointing to Jesus sacrificing himself on the cross in love, refusing to seek violence or vengeance. Essentially what this passage is conveying is that Jesus has conquered and is victorious, but the way he conquers is distinct from the way we do. As Richard Bauckham reinforces, "That the slaughtered Lamb is on the throne makes the sacrificial death of Jesus Christ the key to how God rules the world."[19] The lion never appears again, but the lamb remains a prominent theme.

I'm obviously just scratching the surface of this complicated book, but for our purposes here I simply want to make a point. Revelation is not teaching a violent, blood thirsty Jesus, contradicting whom we see in the Gospels. That would be the epitome of an anti-Christ, and if Revelation were teaching that, it would not belong in our New Testament canon.[20] These issues were exactly why the early church was slow to admit and incorporate this book with the rest of the New Testament. In the end, the last thing we should do is use the most complicated and confusing book in the New Testament to override the clear portrait of Christ we have in the Gospels.

No one knows the Father like the Son, and Jesus speaks of a heavenly Father whom we can trust. He doesn't fly off the handle, or write us off when we screw up. He is kind, patient, and merciful.

INTO THE DEPTHS

Jesus reveals the character of the Father to us, most profoundly on the cross. This is not because God was pouring violence on his Son, but instead because Jesus submitted to *our* violence and darkness to show us how far God is willing to go to love us. On the cross our scapegoating tendencies were shown for what they were. Jesus went into the depths of our sin and still cried out for forgiveness. He took our worst and responded in love.

This is how love speaks to us when and where we need it. We need to know that we are valued for who we are, and that our darkness cannot change that. This is why committed relationships can be so healing. It is also why they can be so painful. Intimate relationships require going to the

---

18. Rev 5:6 (NRSV).

19. Bauckham, "The Language of Warfare," 34.

20. This might sound very backwards. We need to keep in mind that the New Testament canon was chosen in such a way as to be faithful to the faith tradition of the church, going back to Jesus Christ himself. Evangelicals often think of the New Testament canon as preceding tradition, but this ignores the timeline of how the canon was developed.

depths of someone's dysfunctions. It means taking a few jabs. It means being the brunt of lashing out and defense mechanisms. It is the way that people come to see what they are doing, and how hurtful it can be. Sometimes the behaviors are so harmful and damaging that boundaries have to be put in place, and hopefully that action will be a wakeup call. What we really need is for someone to say, "I love you. I see the beauty inside you, and I'm not giving up." This is what Irene and so many others have done for me, and I am so thankful. This is the heart of the Gospel for us. We have been embraced in Christ, and no matter how much we act out, he's never letting go.

Unfortunately, many Christians have been taught to be terrified of God. This is our "play it safe" approach. We often go through our lives with a sense of dread at what God is capable of if we fail. The irony is that we call this faith. This is the opposite of what Jesus offers us. Jesus invites us to a much grander and liberating story. Growing up in church circles we were often influenced by this unspoken question, "What would happen if we die and find out God is harsher than we thought?" That's a question that drives many people's lives, and which haunts their mental landscapes. It is not, however, a question that is fitting for the good news of Jesus. His good news is better. What if we encountered the faith to ask a more stirring question: "How would we live if we truly got a glimpse of how good God is, and how dotingly he looks upon us?" Imagine the possibilities.

CHAPTER 9

Your Sacrifice Is No Good Here

I LOVE HISTORY. IF I had time I could watch historical documentaries for hours and hours. I am very intrigued by past civilizations, including the Mesoamerican cultures from centuries ago. One of the prominent features in many of those civilizations was their sacrificial system and the towering temples and pyramids on which they were performed.

Sacrifice was not relegated to these cultures, however, but "has been a feature of virtually every human civilization."[1] The purpose of sacrifice varied but often was used to curry favor with the gods.

The gods of the ancient world were often unpredictable. Their character was similar to humans. Therefore, people often struggled to know where they stood with the gods. In an attempt to remedy this, the ancients would offer sacrifices. Sometimes the sacrifices were to appease the gods, sometimes to thank them, but always to stay on their good side.

The practice of sacrifice in the Old Testament, therefore, is not completely unique. As Peter Enns explains, "The Old Testament world was a world of temples, priests, and sacrifice. Israel was not the first nation, nor the last, to have a religious system centered on temples, priests, and sacrifice. Such things were woven into the fabric of the ancient societies of the Mesopotamian world."[2]

On the surface, it seems that the Hebrew God is just like the rest of the ancient gods. He often seems arbitrary and bloodthirsty. There are rituals that one has to go through in order to come close to his presence. Life has to

1. Heim, *Saved from Sacrifice*, 39.

2. Enns, *Inspiration*, 7.

be given, blood has to be poured, and it has to be done in the precise manner in order to satisfy this deity. He seems pretty cranky and irritable—far from the kind of God we could call Abba.

This is one way to look at it, but perhaps we misunderstand God's intentions. Perhaps God was acting in an incarnational way even then. We can see this as God works with Abram.

Sacrifice was the way people lived in the ancient world, so when God begins speaking to Abram about his promises—how he will bless him, and bless the world, and give him descendants—and he asks Abram to get animals for sacrifice, Abram knows exactly what to do with them. He's not turned off by the request because that's how the world worked at that time. Without needing instructions, Abram cuts the animals in half. In that time this was how one made an agreement with someone else. Cut the animals in half, spread the halves out, and the two parties would walk between them as a way to say, "May my life be taken as well if I break the agreement."

What happens next would have been completely unexpected. Abram falls into a trance in which God speaks to him. God tells him about his descendants, how numerous they will be, what they will go through, and the land they will inherit. To seal the deal God, in the form of a smoking firepot, goes between the animals by himself. God seals the deal for them both. Here is a God who offers everything instead of demanding it from us.

There is a gradual moving away from sacrifice, very gradual. It has to be, because as a species we don't take change very well. We see a bit of this change taking place later in the Abraham story. In chapter 22 God commands Abraham to offer up his son as a sacrifice. Once again, Abraham knows what to do; that's how it worked. For a moment, this God looks like all the other gods—blood-thirsty and ritualistic. Once again an unexpected twist occurs. God calls it off and provides his own sacrifice. In the midst of this barbaric story is a glimpse of a new understanding of God breaking through; a God who will not accept human sacrifice.

If we look at these stories as a textbook on what God always looks like, we end up with a dysfunctional faith. Rob Bell, as he so often does, puts it succinctly: "You find these stories violent and repulsive and barbaric because they are. If you didn't find them shocking and awful and confusing, something is wrong with you. And people who read these stories and say, well, that's just how God is, have a very, very warped and dangerous view of God."[3]

That kind of reading of scripture is where the monster in the closet gets its fuel. If the Father of Jesus can demand child sacrifice, isn't he like all the

3. Bell, *What Is the Bible,* 122.

other gods? (And how do we explain him offering his own Son as a sacrifice? More on that later).

We continue on in the story and see a God who seems to stipulate a system of sacrifice for his people. Isn't this just like all the gods of all the other nations? It seems that way, but the motivation behind it is different. This system is offered so the people can approach God and get close to Him. This is the opposite of other systems, and definitely the opposite of the monster in my closet. In a world where people were used to offering sacrifices and never knowing when enough is enough, this system offers a way to be at peace and have assurance that we are okay with God. Is it God's desire for people to sacrifice animals and go through rituals to be with him? No, but sacrifice was what they knew, and God is getting through to them, so that their way of understanding God becomes less harsh.

The bottom line is that sacrifice is our invention, not God's. His grace weaves through the lives of the Hebrews so that they take a step forward. A system of sacrifice develops that is more compassionate than had previously existed.

Eventually though, as it often does, the system became the point. The elements of compassion faded away. God's true desires, however, will become more apparent over time. God doesn't desire sacrifice, and gradually this message starts to come through.

Passages in scripture start to undermine the sacrificial system. Some outright reject it.

For example, Samuel tells Saul, "To obey is better than sacrifice, and to heed than the fat of rams."[4] The priority of sacrifice is lower in this passage.

In Psalm 51, David grieves over his terrible moral failure and includes this sentiment,

> "You do not delight in sacrifice, or I would bring it; you do not take pleasure in burnt offerings. My sacrifice, O God, is a broken spirit; a broken and contrite heart you, God, will not despise."[5]

This message gets even more explicit, as in Jeremiah:

> "Thus says the Lord of hosts, the God of Israel: Add your burnt offerings to your sacrifices, and eat the flesh. For in the day that I brought your ancestors out of the land of Egypt, I did not speak to them or command them concerning burnt offerings and sacrifices. But this command I gave them, 'Obey my voice, and I

---

4. 1 Sam 15:22 (NIV).

5. Ps 51:16-17 (NIV).

will be your God, and you shall be my people; and walk only in
the way that I command you, so that it may be well with you."[6]

And finally, the Old Testament passage that Jesus quoted more than any
other, "I desire mercy, not sacrifice."[7] Jesus is revealing where God has truly
shown through and builds on it.

When he assures the crowd that he has come to fulfill the law, he
doesn't mean that he's simply going to go along with everything that was
written and asserted about God. He can't mean that, since shortly after he
will begin teaching, "You have heard it said . . . but I say to you."

Eventually Jesus would make an even grander gesture when he entered
the temple and "began to drive out all the people buying and selling animals
for sacrifice. He knocked over the tables of the money changers and the
chairs of those selling doves. He said to them, "The Scriptures declare, 'My
Temple will be called a house of prayer,' but you have turned it into a den of
thieves!'"[8]

The passage from Isaiah that Jesus references speaks of God's including
all people in his kingdom, but the temple had become a source of exclusion.
To combat this, Jesus heals the blind and disabled in the temple, people who
previously were not allowed within the temple walls.

In the temple scene Jesus also refers back to Jeremiah in a speech where
the Old Testament prophet foretells of the temple's destruction. So Jesus is
not trying to reform the temple, but actually claiming that the temple and
the entire sacrificial enterprise that resides there must stop. Thus he forces
the sacrificial animals out and tosses the tables aside. Hardin puts it this
way:

"This is not a story about Jesus getting mad; it is the great prophetic
act that the end of all sacrifice had come, that something new, mercy and
compassion, replaced sacrifice, which were far more pleasing to God than
the blood of bulls and goats."[9]

To recap: in the ancient world people never knew where they stood
with the gods. They often used life circumstances such as wealth, health, and
military strength to determine whether the gods were for them or against
them. They also used sacrificial systems to try and ensure divine favor.
Through his actions, particularly in this temple scene, Jesus is communicating the message that God was always trying to get across: sacrifice is not
necessary because God is always for you.

6. Jer 7:21-23 (NRSV).

7. Hos 6:6 (NIV).

8. Matt 21:12-13 (NLT).

9. Hardin, *Jesus Driven Life,* 1990.

This may not seem like a very important point to make. After all, we don't have sacrificial systems as an option anymore—not in the traditional way. The problem is that the God many Christians confess is just as moody and fickle as the gods of the ancient world. We need a way to appease him. For many Christians, therefore, the religious duties became a form of sacrifice.

Church attendance became one area of sacrifice. Pastors and parishioners alike often stretch themselves paper thin doing everything involved in keeping a church running. There is often much guilt involved. At times this has led to immense inner tension, splintered communities, and shattered marriages. It's immensely tragic.

We analyze our amount of Bible reading, our faithfulness to tithing, or our ability to live moral lives to ensure that we are sacrificing enough. But we never really know where the line is. This naturally produces anxiety. We know we're not supposed to feel anxious though, so the guilt continues to mount. The cycle never ends—until we realize that the process of sacrifice and appeasement is not really what God is after.

God does not need any sacrifice or offering in order to look favorably and lovingly toward us. That is why Paul could write in Romans 8, "If God is for us, who is against us? He who did not withhold his own Son, but gave him up for all of us, will he not with him also give us everything else?"[10]

The ancients never knew where they stood with God. Therefore Paul is asserting a revolutionary notion in this passage. God is for us, all the time, sacrifice or no sacrifice. Furthermore, God is not for just some people or certain groups, but gave up his Son for us all.

This is such a foundation shifter for me. I'm still wrestling with the ramifications. But it assures me that through thick and thin, through happy days and depressed days, God's favor toward me does not change. I can approach him, being confident that his love never wavers.

A NEW MODE OF EXISTENCE

"For God has imprisoned all in disobedience so that he may be merciful to all,"[11] Paul says in Romans chapter 11. Paul had a unique calling in his life. He was a messenger to non-Jewish folks, or Gentiles, about the salvation and mercy that was offered to them from Yahweh through his son Jesus.

This was a unique calling because most Jews did not think of their faith as embracing all people, tribes, and nations. But here is Paul writing to Romans, the oppressors of the Jews, filling them in on what God has done.

10. Rom 8:31-32 (NRSV).
11. Rom 11:23 (NRSV).

Paul tells his readers that his people have been stubborn toward God. Many of them, he says, are enemies of God's expanding salvation among the rest of the world. They don't understand the universality of God's love. On the surface, it almost appears that God has given up on them and has chosen the Gentiles instead.

Paul wants to correct this assumption. He doesn't want anyone to get the idea that God chooses people because they are better or more deserving than anyone else. The truth is all of us have hang-ups and rubbish in our lives. We all can be stubborn and hard-hearted at times. And so Paul tells them, "For God has imprisoned all in disobedience so that he may be merciful to all." Everybody screws up, but it's okay. In the end it only awakens us to our need for God's mercy, and his eagerness to offer it.

Paul is so moved and overwhelmed by the thought of God's love that he bursts out with this spontaneous blessing,

> "O the depth of the riches and wisdom and knowledge of God! How unsearchable are his judgments and how inscrutable his ways! For who has known the mind of the Lord? Or who has been his counselor? Or who has given a gift to him, to receive a gift in return? For from him and through him and to him are all things. To him be the glory forever. Amen."[12]

In light of this mercy that God bestows, Paul offers a new way to approach faith and spirituality to begin chapter 12, "I appeal to you therefore, brothers and sisters, by the mercies of God, to present your bodies as a living sacrifice, holy and acceptable to God, which is your spiritual worship."[13]

Paul brings up sacrifice, but in a new way that's not very sacrificial at all, at least not in the way the ancients were used to. No animals, no blood, no altars. Instead, just your everyday lives are desired. I love how Eugene Peterson phrases this verse,

> "So here's what I want you to do, God helping you: Take your everyday, ordinary life—your sleeping, eating, going-to-work, and walking-around life—and place it before God as an offering. Embracing what God does for you is the best thing you can do for him."[14]

Ancient people were always wondering how much sacrifice was enough, and we often do too. Have I lived well enough, generously enough, been kind enough, connected enough? We become unsure of ourselves, our

12. Rom 11:33-36 (NRSV).

13. Rom 12:1 (NRSV).

14. Rom 12:1 (MSG).

status in God's eyes, and seek to right the ship. Remember, sacrifice is our invention, not God's.

So when we are tempted to revert to the older mindset, Paul offers this new mode. We can simply offer our everyday lives to God. Just do the best we can to trust him and to be the people he's created us to be. We'll trip and fall. We'll make mistakes and forget who we are at times. We'll get confused. We'll wonder why we even bother. But we can keep on going. No matter how bad we screw up, God will not give up. We can take the next step, because God truly is for us.

CHAPTER 10

It Happens

I LOVE THUNDERSTORMS. IRENE didn't always share my affection for them. I learned this pretty early in our relationship, on our first date, in fact. It was a few weeks after we started college. We were waiting on the porch of her dormitory to go to a movie, swinging back and forth in the rocking chairs, when a thunderstorm started rolling in. As a native Californian, Irene had seldom experienced a true Midwestern thunderstorm. She started to tense up and question whether we should go out or not. I, on the other hand, was perfectly comfortable. The flashes and subsequent rumblings of these storms are incredibly calming to me. They're one of the features I miss most about living in the Midwest.

I imagine that they scared me some when I was little, when I wasn't familiar with them and didn't know about weather patterns. We were told as children that the thunder was the sound of God bowling, and, of course, we were innocent enough to believe it for a time. Some might find it odd now, but attributing events, whether good or bad, to divine activity has a long history.

This goes all the way back to how the ancients thought of the world. Everything had a reason. It was the gods who were in control, so whatever happened, whether good or evil, was attributed to the gods. If a fellow's day was going well, or his crop yielded an abundant supply, it had to be because the gods were pleased with him. On the other hand, if he was getting sick or facing difficult situations, it was assumed to be because he had made the gods angry. That, as mentioned before, was where sacrifice came into play.

As a new understanding of the divine worked its way through the He-brew people, and they came to believe more and more that there was only one God, they still held onto their understanding that whatever happened, whether good or bad, God did it. So we see that some rather shady things are attributed to God throughout scripture.

One story that always bothered me comes from the book of 2 Samuel. David has decided to bring the Ark of the Covenant to be with him in Jerusalem and travels with his men to retrieve it. They set the ark on a cart pulled by oxen and set off to return home. They are not traveling on a freshly paved street, so there could be some bumps on the way. At one point the oxen stumble, and to keep the ark from falling off the cart, a man named Uzzah grabs ahold of it to keep it from falling. Scripture then tells us, "The Lord's anger burned against Uzzah because of his irreverent act; therefore God struck him down, and he died there beside the ark of God."[1] Even David got a little angry afterwards. It just seems so wrong. But he eventually comes to terms with it, because if it happened, it must have been God's doing.

Later in David's life he gets caught up in some very disturbing behavior. He uses his power as king to sleep with someone else's wife. When he finds out she is pregnant, he calls for her husband, one of his soldiers, to come home and sleep with his wife to make it look as though he is the father. The husband, being an honorable man, refuses to sleep with his wife while all his brothers in arms remain on the battlefield. In turn, David arranges for the husband to be killed in battle and for it to look like an accident.

It's all pretty disturbing, and a reminder that leaders abusing their power is nothing new. God is said to take a tragic situation and make it worse, however, because his way of punishing David is by killing the child that is to be born. An innocent child dies, and it is attributed to God. Because if something happens, God must have done it.

There was an understanding among the ancients that if they were experiencing difficulties or suffering of some kind, it was a way for the gods to punish some offense they had committed. That was one of the points of sacrifice; they could try and appease the god they had angered.

This understanding becomes a foundation of the Torah: "If you fully obey the Lord your God . . . all these blessings will come on you . . . however, if you do not obey the Lord your God . . . all these curses will come on you."[2] Therefore, if you experience difficulties, such as famine or sickness, it must be because you disobeyed God.

There is an element of truth, of course, to the idea that living well will bring you benefits. If we live ethical lives, if we treat others as we would want to be treated, if we work hard and live a disciplined life, we will reap

1. 2 Sam 6:7 (NIV).
2. Deut 28:1-2, 15 (NIV).

the benefits. In general, we will be treated well by others. In general, we will be more rewarded for our hard work than someone who is lazy and undisciplined. But the reality is that ethical people suffer too; kind people get taken advantage of too; hard working people get stepped on by others too.

This truth comes out through the Old Testament text in many areas. One obvious place is the book of Job. Job is afflicted by the death of family members, servants, livestock, and excruciating sores all over his body. His friends come by to comfort him and encourage him to accept the obvious: the only reason he could be suffering is that he has offended God in some way. One friend asks Job, "Think now, who that was innocent ever perished? Or where were the upright cut off?"[3] But Job will not give in; he insists there is no good reason for God to treat him this way.

Other writers in scripture look around and notice the inconsistency. Jeremiah complains, "You are always righteous, Lord, when I bring a case before you. Yet I would speak with you about your justice: Why does the way of the wicked prosper? Why do all the faithless live at ease?"[4] The Psalmist moans a similar grumble: "The Lord is a God who avenges. O God who avenges, shine forth. Rise up, Judge of the earth; pay back to the proud what they deserve. How long, Lord, will the wicked, how long will the wicked be jubilant?"[5]

Bad things happen. The rules of the game are not so evenly applied. So is God suspect? Does he arbitrarily reward some and afflict others? That is the question. Over time, however, a development of understanding takes place that another power is at work. God is not the only one moving (besides us and our own destructive ways, of course). We can see this in the book of Job as the prologue describes the conversation between Satan and God. This development of Satan begins as God's prosecuting attorney, but over time he becomes separate. If God is good, people gradually realize, he cannot be the source of evil.

We see this development as well in another story from 2 Samuel. David decides to count his soldiers to see how strong his army is. In doing so, he shows that he trusts his resources more than God, and he cares more about looking like the other powers around him than remaining faithful.

David later realizes what he has done. He confesses his sin to God, and in return God punishes the nation with a plague.[6] What's odd is that,

---

3. Job 4:7 (NRSV).

4. Jer 12:1 (NIV).

5. Ps 94:1-3 (NIV).

6. There are a few things in this story that seem odd to us. One is the fact that God is said to punish an entire nation for the sin of one man. In that time it was an accepted belief that the king represented the people of a given nation, meaning that the people

in this story, we are told that it is God himself who actually incited David to commit this sin. When this story is told again in 1 Chronicles, however, it reports Satan as the one who caused David to act in this way. An understanding is developing. If evil has been committed, God could not have caused it, because God is good.

One other example comes from the Exodus story. The foundation of the Exodus is breathtaking and revolutionary, namely that God is opposed to the powerful in defense of the oppressed. That said, there are a few concerning moments in this story, not least of which is the final plague against Egypt. God is said to kill the firstborn of the entire nation. Infants and toddlers lose their lives in this final act, leaving countless mourners in its wake. Over time, however, there is apparently some concern over attributing this to God. This can be seen in the book of Jubilees, which, as Derek Flood points out, "attributes this to "the powers of Mastema" which literally means in Hebrew "the powers of Hate" (Jubilees 49:2). This illustrates the shift in thinking that was occurring within Judaism at the time which recognized the obvious moral difficulty in attributing acts of evil to God."[7]

Asserting that God is love, and yet commits atrocities on par with Hitler, Stalin, and others, makes God (to borrow a phrase from John Wesley) out to be "worse than the devil."[8] We really don't need a devil if this is how God operates, and because the ancients attributed everything to God, they didn't need the devil either. God becomes someone around whom we must walk on eggshells because we don't know what side of the bed he woke up on this morning. This is not the Abba of whom Jesus speaks.

A development was underway, and it would find culmination in Jesus Christ.

In Jesus's biggest recorded speech, the Sermon on the Mount, he addresses an issue concerning the kingdom of God and says, "You have heard that it was said, 'Love your neighbor and hate your enemy.'"[9] The Leviticus passage that he is referencing doesn't actually say "hate your enemy," but this was the unspoken understanding of many Jews. They would love their fellow Jews (although, like most of us, they weren't very good at that either), but they were often ready to cast off anyone else. This was, after all, how God appears to operate in parts of the Old Testament. Of course, there were many words of mercy as well, such as God commanding his people to accept

---

could suffer for his lack of morality as well as receive blessings for his righteousness. This was simply part of their worldview in that time.

7. Flood, *Disarming Scripture*, 102.

8. Wesley, "Sermon 128," part VII, section 2.

9. Matt 5:43 (NIV).

the foreigner because they knew what it was like to be foreigners in Egypt. But it was much easier to latch on to the passages of wrath, exclusion, and vengeance, not knowing that it was their own people's sinful tendencies that led them to portray God in such a way.

Why would they love their enemies when their God never did? That's where Jesus confronts them with a new paradigm. He tells them to love their enemies, so "that you may be children of your Father in heaven. He causes his sun to rise on the evil and the good, and sends rain on the righteous and the unrighteous."[10] Jesus portrays a different image of God, one who treats everyone with the same dignity and grace. Righteous, wicked, friend, enemy, all are treated the same in his kingdom. God treats us, not as our behavior deserves, but in a way that is faithful to his character.

Many of the Jews didn't understand this; many of us still don't. The prevailing thought was that any pain or hardship was afflicted by God. Thus they assumed that one would only suffer if they had offended him. On one occasion Jesus and his disciples encountered a man who was born blind. Stuck in their way of seeing the world, the disciples asked him, "Why was this man born blind? Was it because of his own sins or his parents' sins?"[11] Jesus corrects them, telling them it's not about punishment at all, but now it's an opportunity for God's healing to take place.

On another occasion people reported to Jesus about some Galileans who had been killed by Pilate in the temple. Jesus confronts them with their typical way of thinking and asks, "Do you think that because these Galileans suffered in this way they were worse sinners than all other Galileans? No, I tell you; but unless you repent, you will all perish as they did."[12] God doesn't send calamities on people. We shouldn't focus on their behavior, but should focus on ourselves, ensuring that our selfishness and egos don't take us down the wrong path. We tend to shoot ourselves in the foot, and God wants to help us with that.[13]

This ancient inclination to attribute all things to God has not died. Some prominent religious leaders are quick to pounce on a tragedy as an

10. Matt 5:45 (NIV).

11. John 9:2 (NLT).

12. Luke 13:2-3 (NRSV).

13. It is important to remember the backdrop of the Roman occupation and the political tension surrounding it. Pilate's actions in the temple may very well have been the response of a violent oppressor towards a people who often sought national rebellion against him. So when Jesus warns against perishing here, he is not speaking of going to hell or being rejected by God. Instead, he is speaking of the desire of many Jews to overthrow their occupiers, the endless cycle of violence that ensues, and the destructive pattern of violence in general. As Jesus warned Peter, "all who draw the sword will die by the sword." (Matt 26:52 NIV)

opportunity to explain God's punishments. Hurricanes, earthquakes, and any other disasters we can think of are often blamed on some sin committed by the victims. Some Christians, during the time of hurricane Katrina, explained the disaster as God's wrath against the locals, all the while refusing to use the same thought process to explain their own problems and difficulties. I have even had people tell me they would never consider living in San Francisco because they believe that at any time God will punish the LGBT community there by sending an earthquake that sends them off into the ocean. Needless to say, this way of interpreting events around us is still very much present.

These sentiments also continue on a more individual level as well. Unhelpful comments are made when death occurs tragically. "God just needed another angel in heaven." This of course implies that God was the one who orchestrated the car crash or disease that took the loved one. To be fair, we also praise God when a life is spared. "Someone up there must like her," the colloquial saying goes. It begs the question though: Does that mean God dislikes anyone who suffers?

The confusing and difficult reality is that God has created a universe where bad things can happen. Fires break out. Earthquakes strike. Tornados and hurricanes devastate. It happens.

While these tragedies cannot be attributed to humans, there is an untold amount of suffering that does come from our hands. Wars, slavery, torture, racism, and inequality are all from our design. I can make my case that I'm not to blame because I've never murdered, or raped, or enslaved. The truth is, however, that I've done plenty to hurt those around me. Sometimes I have hate or bitterness in my heart. This isn't a self-deprecating moment; it's just the reality. I'm grateful for the grace I've received from Jesus and from the ones I love.

We can ask the question, why does God allow these things? Why didn't he cure all the diseases, secure all the hydroplaning cars, and feed all the hungry? Why does he let us treat each other so badly?

God apparently makes space for our baggage in his universe. That may seem troubling, but the reality is that God had to do this even for our universe to be possible. If God is all present, that is, everywhere all the time, then the only way for there to be space for us is for God to diminish or empty himself. There is a word for this emptying in scripture: *kenosis*. It describes the kind of love God lavishes as he gives of himself for others. Brad Jersak puts it this way, describing Simone Weil's view on creation, "In the beginning, out of his fullness, the Creator emptied himself— kenosis!—to make space for creation so that we could authentically live and move and have being."[14]

This *kenosis* was not a one-time act in creation. Instead, it is the word that Paul uses to describe the incarnation—Jesus becoming human. "Christ Jesus, who, though he was in the form of God, did not regard equality with God as something to be exploited, but emptied (*kenosis*) himself, taking the form of a slave, being born in human likeness."[15]

Here's what is truly astonishing. God emptied himself to create the universe. When we screw things up with our violence and selfishness, God doesn't give up. Rather, he empties himself again in Christ to enter into our mess and bring healing and restoration. Paul even says at one point that Jesus brings everything to the Father so that he will be "all in all."[16] Apparently this God who empties himself to create us also finds a way to bring us fully into him. This sounds like Jesus when he envisions, "On that day you will know that I am in my Father, and you in me, and I in you."[17]

We can wonder why God makes space for the suffering in the world, but we can also marvel at the absurd amount of patience and undying love he has in order never to give up. The truth is that I would not know what love is unless those closest to me made space to be affected by my crap, my pain, and my annoying, sometimes hurtful behaviors. I would guess that the same is true for most of us.

When we are in these close, intimate, and vulnerable relationships, we often have an internal clock going. We are calculating when our next mess up will be our last and the relationship will end. When we interpret every pain, frustration, and tragedy as God's judgment on us, that internal clock ticks for God too. Has God finally had enough? Has he reached his limit and decided I'm no longer worth his time? Jesus's union with us tells us otherwise.

LET US NOT GROW WEARY

Bad things do happen, many times to people who bring honor and beauty to the world. Civil rights leaders get assassinated. Children die of hunger. Friends who are much too young are afflicted with awful diseases. It just

14. Jersak, *Christlike God*, 128. Taken from *A More Christlike God*, by Brad Jersak. Copyright ©2015 by Plain Truth Ministries/CWRpress. Used by permission of Plain Truth Ministries, www.ptm.org

15. Phil 2:5-7 (NRSV).

16. 1 Cor 15:28 (NRSV).

17. John 14:20 (NRSV).

doesn't make any sense sometimes. Sometimes, we have to have the courage to go on fighting, not knowing what's going to come around the corner. After all, as Paul says, we are destined for "good works."[18] We are created to make a positive difference in the world around us.

In Galatians Paul encourages his people, "So let us not grow weary in doing what is right, for we will reap at harvest time, if we do not give up. So then, whenever we have an opportunity, let us work for the good of all, and especially for those of the family of faith."[19]

It sounds sort of odd to talk about growing weary of doing what's right, but we've all experienced it. Sometimes the pain and suffering in the world make working for good overwhelming. Other times we get chastised by the very ones we try to help, and it can feel pointless.

What can make it worse, however, is if we interpret any onslaught against us as God punishing us. Then it feels like there's no winning with him. This is precisely why I wanted to kick God out of my life. It seemed like I could never placate his temper. Thankfully, the reality is much different. It's important to remember that, through it all, God has not changed his mind about us.

We need an honesty about everything that happens around us, without the added weight of shame and anxiety that comes from seeing it as God's anger toward us. We also need hope to keep moving forward, trusting that God is still good. He is ever at work in ways we don't understand.

This is part of the message flowing from the cross. The Father loves Jesus, and yet the Son is called to faithfulness, all the way to the cross. God does not exempt himself from our suffering. After the crucifixion, the situation looks like devastation and despair. Every one of Jesus's disciples gives up, assuming his death signals the end of their lives with him. But it's not the end. Not even close. Instead, the Father shows that he can bring good out of even the greatest tragedy.

If we see every pain, every heartache, and every inconvenience in life as a possible venue for God's punishment, we will question God's presence in our lives. We will also be unable to see the potential for meaning and purpose in the midst of every circumstance.

God doesn't inflict suffering upon us. Instead, he uses each and every factor in our lives as opportunities for enlightenment and restoration. The reality is that so much of our suffering is self-inflicted, and each new stub of the toe gives us a chance to see that perhaps we need a little more light. The suffering that cannot be blamed on our own individual or collective choices

18. Eph 2:10 (NRSV).

19. Gal 6:9-10 (NRSV).

often brings to light the dysfunctional and self-serving ways we cope. Seeing these with new eyes can lead us to letting go. Suddenly, we can find meaning through all of reality, because we tap into that which is deeper and cannot be altered or diminished.

It begins to make sense why Paul would write in Romans 5, "We also boast in our sufferings, knowing that suffering produces endurance, and endurance produces character, and character produces hope, and hope does not disappoint us, because God's love has been poured into our hearts through the Holy Spirit that has been given to us."[20]

When we get to the end of ourselves, we are left with hope for only what God can do, and we find that he is always there, always comes through, and is always on our side.

Jesus reminds us, "I have said this to you, so that in me you may have peace. In the world you face persecution. But take courage; I have conquered the world!"[21] Sometimes life can feel like getting dashed against the rocks. We must remember that God is not the one behind it. He hasn't turned on us, or forsaken us. When I have been taught otherwise, it has contributed to a debilitating anxiety. How can I possibly have courage to move forward if God has written me off?

But that is not the story. That is not reality. We must exit the cave, as Plato might put it, and discover what's really going on. Jesus has conquered so that in the midst of all the pain and confusion, we can experience his enduring peace. Take courage.

20. Rom 5:3-5 (NRSV).
21. John 16:33 (NRSV).

PART III

CONFRONTED WITH OUR ILLUSIONS

CHAPTER 11

For God Was So Angry
That He Killed His Only Son

I DON'T DO WELL with tense situations, particularly if the cause is relationship conflict that includes angry yelling. As far as fight or flight goes, I'm definitely a runner. If there is a clash or argument going on around me, I'm looking for all the available exits. If it's directed at me, I often just say whatever I think the person wants to hear just to find a conclusion. That's often how I survived being a pastor's kid.

My wife is just the opposite. She's a fighter. That's her survival mode. When she's put in that position, she is a force of nature. You can probably guess how many of our early relationship conflicts went down. She fought, and I fled.

This is part of our survival mechanism as a species. If something stressful and dangerous occurs, our instincts take over. This is beneficial when we are facing such a situation. It is detrimental, however, to relationships as well as general psychological health.

We can see this in people who have experienced trauma. They have strong memories of what happened to them to make sure they can be on the lookout for it in the future. If they are triggered, if something in their environment brings back those memories, their survival mode kicks in. I remember one night when this happened at work. I was working at a pizza place, and several pizzas were going through the oven. Unfortunately that was the moment the oven decided to stop working. When the pizzas came out, they were a little undercooked, but I really didn't notice. I'm not the most observant person. When my boss saw them, he yelled at me and couldn't understand how I didn't catch the problem. I completely froze. I was so tense. I just shut down and became silent. Later that night I broke down crying. At the time I didn't understand very well about triggers and trauma, so I had no clue why I was responding that way. We react in different ways to environments that are dangerous or that trigger past trauma. Others in my shoes may very well have responded by screaming back at my boss and losing control of their anger.

Threatening situations are not conducive to healthy relationships, constructive conversations, or trust building. While I'm no expert on how the brain works, I do understand, from others smarter than I am, that there is a neurological explanation for this. Our brains have different regions with different responsibilities. The prefrontal cortex is responsible for much of what makes up our personality. It's also how we reason and think clearly. The amygdala in our brain is responsible for the emotions that have to do with survival mechanisms, like fight or flight.

What happens in a threatening situation is that the amygdala takes over. Our prefrontal cortex, which gives us our ability to reason and makes up our personality, then goes completely out the window. Daniel Goleman, in his book *Emotional Intelligence,* refers to these moments as "neural hijackings." As he explains, "The amygdala's extensive web of neural connections allows it, during an emotional emergency, to capture and drive much of the rest of the brain-including the rational mind."[1] Tense situations can stir up the emotions in us that "hijack" our ability to analyze and process. Goleman elaborates, "The prefrontal cortex is the brain region responsible for working memory. But circuits from the limbic brain to the prefrontal lobes mean that the signals of strong emotion-anxiety, anger, and the like-can create neural static, sabotaging the ability of the prefrontal lobe to maintain working memory. This is why when we are emotionally upset we say we "just can't think straight"-and why continual emotional distress can create deficits in a child's intellectual abilities, crippling the capacity to learn."[2]

Tense situations can happen, and our fight or flight system is an essential tool. However, in cases where the threats and stress are a constant presence, they can have devastating effects on our ability to think, as well as our general ability to truly experience the world around us for what it is.

Why am I talking about this? If threatening situations or conversations have the power to shut down our ability to think straight and to be present, what do you think happens when someone hears a "turn or burn" message about the Gospel? What happens when we are told that God's fundamental

1. Goleman, *Emotional Intelligence,* 17.
2. Ibid, 27.

attitude toward us is anger and wrath? In this case the stress becomes a constant presence. Could there be anything more threatening than to hear that the all-powerful being in the universe put a hit out on you? But thank God that Jesus took the hit instead, right?

This is the way that many Evangelicals view what is happening on the cross. God is angry with us because of our sin and needs justice. Apparently justice means death, and so he wants to go after us. Instead, Jesus offers to be punished in our place. God the Father ends up looking more like the Godfather.[3]

Even if we accept the Gospel message and decide to follow Jesus, the threatening messages often do not end there. In certain circles we are also told that if we are not faithful to our new commitment, that God will still end up throwing us in the fire.

The trouble is that the concept of being faithful to Jesus can look so different. Some will tell us that believing the right things is what's important. In the end, regardless of how we live our lives, as long as we profess to be "believers" we'll be safe. Jesus becomes less a Lord and more a password to get into Club Paradise.

Others claim that we can't just believe, but we also have to live a life that honors Jesus. It's a great sentiment. Love God, love others, and show compassion to those around us. But how do we know what's enough? What if I could have given a little more money, a little more time, or a little more of myself to those hurting around me?

None of this would be so anxiety inducing if it were not for the backdrop of God's apparent anger problem. Why is this our view of God? Why does anger seem to be such a prominent theme to the evangelical Gospel?

One reason is our apparent obsession with, and misunderstanding of, the "wrath of God." As we looked at scripture earlier, we addressed the issue that God seems so often to be angry about something, and eager to satiate his rage by directing it at someone. The problem is that we tend to read those passages into Jesus instead of the other way around. We also saw that we often miss the way the Old Testament is moving forward, even if it seems backward to us. The result is we can read into the story something that isn't there.

One example of this is the idea that Jesus had to die to satisfy God's anger. We get here by projecting violent images of God onto the cross. We assume that what's going on with the Old Testament law is God's blood thirst being placated. We then project this onto the Gospel.

---

3. Johnson, "Compassionate Eschatology with Michael Hardin."

The evangelical Gospel is often about a God who wants to inflict appeasing punishment onto all of wicked humanity, and a Son who offers us an escape hatch. This punishment is understood to be the wrath of God. It is also what Jesus saves us from when he dies. This is not what the wrath of God is, however, nor is it how sin works.

Sin results in our suffering at our own hands. Maybe we act selfishly at times and see the pain it causes to those around us, and the mistrust it breeds in relationships. Maybe we choose to trust ourselves instead of Jesus and experience the stress and exhaustion of carrying the world on our shoulders. Many biblical writers see this and use a metaphor to describe it. That metaphor is the "wrath of God." As Brian Zhand explains, "When we sin against the two great commandments—to love God with all our heart and to love our neighbor as ourselves—we suffer the inevitable consequences of acting against love. We can call this the wrath of God if we like; the Bible does, but that doesn't mean that God literally loses his temper."[4]

When biblical writers use this language, they seem to be either still in the mindset of attributing everything, even evil, to God, or are using it with the assumption that their readers understand the metaphor.

Though the concept of God's wrath is mentioned in different passages, a significant time in scripture when the "wrath of God" is explained in any way is in Romans chapter 1, where Paul writes, "The wrath of God is being revealed from heaven against all the godlessness and wickedness of people."[5]

What does God do to them to pour out his wrath? He "gave them over in the sinful desires of their hearts . . . to shameful lusts . . . to a depraved mind."[6]

What is the wrath of God, then? It is allowing us to have the painful consequences of our stubborn, selfish ways. It does not define wrath as harsh punishment attributed to God either. But we do, and what's more, we often make this a central aspect of salvation on the cross. We even say that God's wrath was poured out on Jesus for our sake. The problem is that, with a proper understanding of wrath in mind, there's not a single place in scripture that teaches this. Yet it is central to the Gospel of many Christians.

There are a couple of passages that have typically been used to equate the wrath of God with vengeful punishment. Isaiah 52-3 is one in particular: "Surely he has borne our infirmities and carried our diseases; yet we accounted him stricken, struck down by God, and afflicted."[7]

---

4. Zhand, *Sinners in the Hands,* 16.

5. Rom 1:18 (NIV).

6. Rom 1:24, 26, 28 (NIV).

7. Isa 53:4 (NRSV).

We read that Jesus was stricken by God, but we miss that this was our conclusion, not God's. We considered him stricken. We also conclude that God's wrath was poured out on Christ because of Jesus's lament on the cross, "My God, my God, why have you forsaken me."[8] In chapter 3 we looked at how we interpret this passage to mean that God cannot look upon our darkness. We also use this to assert that God abandons those who are in sin. Since we believe that Jesus bore our sin on the cross, we conclude that God's natural response was to abandon Jesus too. But Jesus is referencing a Psalm, the message of which is anything but abandonment. Here is a portion of that Psalm:

> "O my God, I cry by day, but you do not answer; and by night, but find no rest. Yet you are holy, enthroned on the praises of Israel. In you our ancestors trusted; they trusted, and you delivered them. To you they cried, and were saved; in you they trusted, and were not put to shame . . . yet it was you who took me from the womb; you kept me safe on my mother's breast. On you I was cast from my birth, and since my mother bore me you have been my God. Do not be far from me, for trouble is near and there is no one to help . . . I am poured out like water and all my bones are out of joint, my heart is like wax; it is melted within my breast; my mouth is dried up like a potsherd, and my tongue sticks to my jaws; you lay me in the dust of death. For dogs are all around me; a company of evildoers encircles me. My hands and feet have shriveled; I can count all my bones. They stare and gloat over me; they divide my clothes among themselves, and for my clothing they cast lots . . . you who fear the Lord, praise him! All you offspring of Jacob, glorify him; stand in awe of him, all you offspring of Israel! For he did not despise or abhor the affliction of the afflicted; he did not hide his face from me, but heard when I cried to him."[9]

These are the words of a man who is in anguish and desperation, but they are not the words of a man who believes God has abandoned him. Instead this passage is the stubborn refusal to believe that God forsakes us no matter how much suffering we endure. God doesn't punish sin by deserting his children. Instead, the sense of being rejected and cast off is what happens when we live out of our egos instead of our true God-given identities.

God does not pour out wrath on Jesus because that's not what wrath is. Wrath is the natural consequence of sin. Since Jesus lived a life of love and grace without exception, there were no consequences to be had for him.

8. Matt 27:46 (NRSV).

9. Ps 22:2-5, 9-11, 14-18, 23-24 (NRSV).

Instead he suffered the consequence of our sin, our hate, our violence, yet we are the ones who considered him "stricken, struck down by God, and afflicted." That is why it is so damaging to talk of the cross in this way: we are falling into the trap from which the cross is intended to save us in the first place.

Jesus's accusers lived by the same logic and based their persecution of him on it. "He saved others," they said, "but he can't save himself . . . He trusts in God. Let God rescue him now if he wants him."[10] The words "King of the Jews" were hung above his head on the cross, clearly in an effort to mock him, because his suffering was proof to his executioners that he was no such thing. But Paul tells a different story: "Christ redeemed us from the curse of the law by becoming a curse for us—for it is written, "Cursed is everyone who hangs on a tree"[11] Paul is saying that Jesus becomes a curse in our eyes, but comes out triumphantly to show us that our concept of who God blesses and curses is flawed. This challenges our fundamental assumptions, or as Paul put it to the Corinthians, "We proclaim Christ crucified, a stumbling block to Jews and foolishness to Gentiles."[12]

Later Paul would enthusiastically assure the church in Rome,

> "Who will separate us from the love of Christ? Will hardship, or distress, or persecution, or famine, or nakedness, or peril, or sword? As it is written, "For your sake we are being killed all day long; we are accounted as sheep to be slaughtered." No, in all these things we are more than conquerors through him who loved us. For I am convinced that neither death, nor life, nor angels, nor rulers, nor things present, nor things to come, nor powers, nor height, nor depth, nor anything else in all creation, will be able to separate us from the love of God in Christ Jesus our Lord."[13]

Paul lists some of the very things that we are convinced signal God's displeasure with us. Hardship. Distress. Persecution. Hunger. Paul contradicts our usual assumptions about these things, insisting that God still loves us. How can we be assured of this? Because Jesus endured hardship, and persecution, and violent death, but three days later God raised Him. God was still with him.

We need to know that when we hurt, and suffer, and grieve, and strain just to make it to the next day, there is no God who is afflicting us,

10. Matt 27:42-3 (NIV).

11. Gal 3:13 (NRSV).

12. 1 Cor 1:23 (NRSV).

13. Rom 8:35-39 (NRSV).

condemning us, or chastising us. There is only a God who grieves with us, hurts with us, and cries with us. The cross shows us that at no moment are we ever out of God's loving gaze.

And this is important: not even when we screw up, or maybe I should say, especially not when we screw up. That is when we need the love of our true Father the most. We assume he's out to get us, to punish and embarrass us. This is precisely why Adam, Eve, and we run away. We conceive of a God filled with rage, but his only angst comes from the thought of losing us, and seeing us ruined by our destructive decisions. As my friend and mentor Paul Fitzgerald would put it, "God is not angry at you, he is angry for you."

When we see the cross as punishment and anger, we see a merciless beating that was actually meant for us. We end up picturing Jesus's bloodied body as a warning of what could happen to us if we don't fall in line. It's threatening, it's terrorizing, and it completely paralyzes our ability to think clearly or relax in trust. It leaves us in survival mode, and over long periods of time this leads to anxiety, depression, and a whole host of dysfunctions. It's psychologically damaging. This is my story. Many of my struggles with anxiety and depression can be traced directly to this dilemma.

We need to get away from this toxic viewpoint. We need to get away from thinking anger is a centerpiece of God's character. So many times when I or someone else has talked about God's love, another church member will say something like, "Sure God is loving, but don't forget he's also wrathful, or ready to punish, or holy (as if holy has to be something other than love)." I understand the concern, but essentially what they're saying is, "Sure, God's a good guy, but he's also a jerk sometimes, so don't get too comfortable with him, because you never know what you're dealing with."

Apparently we never know which side of the bed God is going to wake up on, and it's maddening. We don't need this kind of tension, and God does not desire it for us. It inhibits our ability to experience peace, love, and kindness—the very things God offers us. It's stressful and debilitating. We already endure so much pain, and there's a world around us that needs love, compassion, and generosity. I've had a much harder time offering these gifts when shackled by this burden.

Michael Hardin points out, "In the only instances in the New Testament where axiomatic statements are made about God (God is _____), God is called 'light' and 'love.'"[14] So let's make this abundantly clear.

God is not wrath.

God is not anger.

God is not hate.

---

14. Hardin, *Jesus Driven Life*, 2267.

God is not vengeance.
God is not violence.
We don't have to fight.
We don't have to flee.
God is here for us.

CHAPTER 12

Death by Participation

IT WAS THE FIRST time meeting with my spiritual director. I had talked to him on the phone briefly before, but that was the extent of our interaction. A good friend of mine had recommended him to me a few months earlier. I was having a difficult time dealing with my anxiety. I had visited with a therapist, but something didn't feel quite right. I have benefited from counseling several times and appreciate the incredible benefits it offers. At that time in my life I knew my anxiety was tied to my approach to spirituality. So there I was sipping on a vanilla latte at Starbucks, trying to explain to my director what I was searching for.

"I want to grow in my identity in Christ and not let others around me dictate who I am. I want to be able to love others unconditionally without sacrificing my identity in the process," I finally explained.

"Is that all?" he replied with a chuckle. There's nothing like a subtle joke to ease the tension.

I continued, "I know I have come a long way. I can see where I want to be, but it's like there's a mysterious barrier blocking my path. No matter how hard I try, I can't get to the other side."

"Maybe you need to stop trying," he remarked. As a lifelong spiritual performer, that didn't exactly make sense. However, it didn't make a lot of sense to me when Jesus said something similar: "Whoever wants to be my disciple must deny themselves and take up their cross and follow me. For whoever wants to save their life will lose it, but whoever loses their life for me will find it."[1]

---

1. Matt 16:24-25 (NIV).

Jesus talks a lot about dying. Richard Rhor asserts that if a spiritual guide is doing her job, she will talk about dying too.[2] But what does that really mean? When I heard Jesus's teaching on this growing up and in college, it usually had one of two messages attached to it. The first was the principle that in following Jesus we must live sacrificially for others. We must give up our time and money in order to serve others and bless them. I get that. It makes sense to me, even if I'm not the best at following through with it.

Others would talk about how we must be ready to literally lose our lives for the sake of the Gospel. They would talk about the Christians who were martyred in the first few centuries of the faith. They would even talk about how many Christians today are persecuted for their faith in other countries around the world. I get that too. It makes sense, but I have yet to experience being persecuted for my faith, so that option doesn't impact me in my day to day life.

Something still seemed to be missing in those explanations, though they made some valid points. As I spoke with my director I began to see what that neglected aspect was.

Jesus came to reveal our true identity. I keep coming back to this because I've found time and time again that if I don't get this right, the rest of my spirituality falls apart. So I seek to remember the truth, as Francois du Toit paraphrases from Colossians,

"It is in Christ that God finds an accurate and complete expression of himself, in a human body! Jesus mirrors our completeness and endorses our true identity. He is I am in us."[3]

Jesus reveals our true identity by mirroring it to us. The problem is that most of our time is spent living outside of who we are and developing thought patterns and behaviors to ward off the pain that ensues. Sometimes this can look like defense mechanisms to prevent rejection. It can look like a persistent pessimism to keep from facing disappointment. These are just a few examples, and we'll explore this more in a later chapter.

In order to move in a healthier direction we must have a proper understanding of what our real difficulty is. The problem is not that we don't have an identity; the problem is we've forgotten what our identity is. Unfortunately, we've revolved much of our faith and religious practices around the former. So much of church practice and culture is about seeking something that we assume we don't already have.

Of course, this only contributes to the problem. It furthers the notion that we have to attend church, read the Bible, and pray in order for God to redeem us, cleanse us, and transform us. All of these practices can be good

2. Rhor, *Falling Upward*, 85.

3. Col 2:9-10 (Mirror).

and healthy. When done with an anxious motive, however, they can drag us deeper into our sense of lack and missing identity.

We need a different vantage point from which to move forward. We need eyes to see. We focus on learning more, more, and more. But when we've been spinning in circles and become entangled in religious dysfunction, we cannot expect to keep twisting in the same direction and magically be set loose.

We don't need to learn as much as we need to unlearn. We don't need to grasp as much as we need to learn the art of letting go.

My particular faith tribe speaks frequently about "living by the Spirit." I spoke of it as well, but frankly, I had no idea what it really meant. I understood God to be someone who withdraws his presence when we mess up. In addition, when I thought of moments where I could experience God's presence, it was usually within the context of being in church, singing worships songs, or in private devotion and prayer time.

Several years back I prayed and told God that I wanted to be able to experience his presence moment by moment. God has been working on that prayer. To move me in that direction, however, God had to dismantle so much of my faith and understanding of his character. I had to unlearn how I was approaching him. What prevented me from experiencing his presence was not my screw ups, but it was my very notion of how faith works.

Moving forward means letting go. We run into another issue here, though, because our concept of letting go doesn't particularly help much. When we want to let go of something, we tend to push it away, ignore it, or pretend it doesn't exist. The irony is that the more drastically we try to reject anything, the more severely we will be tied to it. True letting go requires that we embrace and engage that which is holding us back. We do this because true release only comes when we see clearly. It is like finding a knot in my shoe strings. If I just start trying to pull the strings apart with brute force, I'll make the knot stronger. First, I need to see the formation of the knot. Only then will I know how to proceed.

The addict would have a much easier time quitting if he had a moment of utter and unobstructed clarity into how enslaved he is, as well as how much his habit hurts himself and those around him. I don't mean that he needs to see an infomercial on the dangers of his addiction. I'm talking about an inner seeing that may be obstructed by inner tensions and struggles.

This was my experience with struggles like depression, anxiety, and the role all of this played in my compulsive attachment to pornography. My understanding of sin at the time was that it should be condemned and avoided at all costs. So I fought to ignore and forget it. But I didn't understand the reasons why I even felt drawn to it. As Richard Rhor suggests, we should learn the lessons our sin has to teach us before we get rid of it.[4]

My moment of clarity came when Irene and I journeyed through marriage counseling. Our counselor explained that a common reason men fall prey to pornography is that they are afraid to try real intimacy and risk rejection. Pornography offers an artificial sense of intimacy and requires no risk, no strength, and no courage. That is why I needed to experience acceptance and inner security from God's love.

Until this point I believed I struggled with pornography simply because I was a rotten and terrible person. The irony was it was this very shame that had led me to my destructive behaviors in the first place; thus, beating myself up only added fuel to the fire. My ultimate problem was my inability to accept love and affection from God or anyone else. Trying to avoid my sin kept me blind to this fundamental problem, and inadvertently escalated it.

This pattern is one tendency that Jesus seeks to undermine through the cross. Instead of dismissing our pain and dysfunctions, he bears them to the cross. Unfortunately we've projected our proclivity for avoidance onto the cross. We assert that Jesus bore our sin so that we don't have to, but Jesus taught that we were meant to follow his lead. "If any want to become my followers, let them deny themselves and take up their cross and follow me."[5]

It sounds backwards and maybe even wrong, but Jesus wants to help us bear our sin. This requires a compassion and patience that we can seldom muster. That is why Jesus speaks of not judging. To change, we have to see, and to see we need to have compassion enough not to label or chastise. So Jesus tells us,

> "Do not judge, so that you may not be judged. For with the judgment you make you will be judged, and the measure you give will be the measure you get. Why do you see the speck in your neighbor's eye, but do not notice the log in your own eye? Or how can you say to your neighbor, 'Let me take the speck out of your eye,' while the log is in your own eye? You hypocrite, first take the log out of your own eye, and then you will see clearly to take the speck out of your neighbor's eye."[6]

The reason we can blatantly and casually judge others is that we become blind to what's stirring within us. It is a problem of sight. We like to focus on behaviors. It gives us a pet project. It makes us feel like we're in control. Frankly, it often doesn't require much hard work on our parts. That's

4. Rhor, *Falling Upward*, 61.
5. Matt 16:24 (NRSV).
6. Matt 7:1-5 (NRSV).

because it's only a symptom. Imagine going into the doctor's office because you had severe headaches and nausea. The doctor would ask you questions, examine you and take some tests. After all the poking and prodding, she calls you with the results. "Well, it looks like you are experiencing headaches and nausea." You would probably wonder where this doctor went to school. The symptoms are the easy part. We must go deeper.

Jesus wants us to see our symptoms—our despair, manipulations, insecurities—to take us deeper. At times it feels cruel and harsh. As Richard Rhor acknowledges, "Yes, "the truth will set you free" as Jesus says (John 8:32), but first it tends to make you miserable."[7] It feels like condemnation, but God is not the one doing the condemning. Rather, he is taking us into our self-condemnation so that we can see clearly what is really going on. In fact, it feels like death because our ego and defense mechanisms are being shown for what they are and stripped of their power. We think that's who we really are, so in a very real way there is dying involved. But the truth that Jesus wants us to see and experience is that only through this journey of dying can we truly encounter life.

This is why death and losing our lives are so emphasized. We come to the other side to find out that what we thought was our life was a facade, but it feels so real. This process is vital; thus, Jesus shared with his disciples:

> "The hour has come for the Son of Man to be glorified. Very truly, I tell you, unless a grain of wheat falls into the earth and dies, it remains just a single grain; but if it dies, it bears much fruit. Those who love their life lose it, and those who hate their life in this world will keep it for eternal life. Whoever serves me must follow me, and where I am, there will my servant be also. Whoever serves me, the Father will honor."[8]

As you can imagine, this is not something many of us run after willingly. We don't want to be exposed. We don't want to change. In truth, most people won't even consider this journey until something forces them to. Even then, it's impossibly difficult. But all things, Jesus assures us, are possible with God. That's why trust is vital here. We must trust Jesus to guide us through.

Our understanding of faith and the cross can hinder us in this process. When we see the cross only as something Jesus did for us, we can avoid this journey by simply having faith in what Jesus accomplished. Our faith can be shaky at times, however, which makes us nervous to venture beyond mental certitude and black or white concepts.

---

7. Rhor, *Breathing Under Water*, 30-1.

8. John 12:24-6 (NRSV).

We need a more challenging and robust journey to go down the path that Jesus calls us to. We are not invited to believe in Jesus in a way that completes a transaction; we are called forth to participate in what Jesus has begun in us. Peter awakens our hope with these words:

> "His divine power has given us everything needed for life and godliness, through the knowledge of him who called us by his own glory and goodness. Thus he has given us, through these things, his precious and very great promises, so that through them you may escape from the corruption that is in the world because of lust, and may become participants of the divine nature"[9]

This faith is not about being religious or ritualistic. It's not about a God sending his Son to take our punishment. This is about a God who wants us to participate in his life, his joy, and his love. We have much to die to and to let go of to move in this direction. But sin and death have ultimately been defeated. We get to participate in this victory. We can't do it on our own, however, which is why we need to have the faith of Christ working within us.[10] That's what it's all about: participating in death in order to experience life. This is precisely what Paul speaks of in Galatians 2: "I have been crucified with Christ; and it is no longer I who live, but it is Christ who lives in me."[11]

God is inviting us to participate in his nature. He wants us to come to terms with our true identities. Remember, "Jesus mirrors our completeness and endorses our true identity. He is I am in us." He doesn't want us just to know it, though, but to experience it deeply. This requires going with Jesus to the cross, bearing our sin with him, and allowing what we see and encounter to change us freely and naturally.

The cross looks violent and ugly because it is our sin on display inflicted on Jesus. The cross reveals our sin to us. We want to look away and deny

---

9. 2 Pet 1:3-4 (NRSV).

10. Prominent scholars have argued that passages in scripture that have been translated in the past as speaking of our having "faith in" Christ would instead be better translated as having the "faith of" Christ. What's the big difference? The notion of having faith in Christ often has led to a faith that becomes focused on mentally agreeing with beliefs about Christ. Curtis Freeman explains that our popular evangelical notion of faith "has so objectified the atoning work of Christ in the cross and so abstracted Christ's redeeming work from all human participation that Christians have been reduced to the role of mere spectators." ("Faith of Jesus Christ," 6393) Having the faith of Christ means that his very life can be active within us through the Spirit because God has embraced humanity in him. As Paul proclaimed in Galatians, "It is no longer I who live, but it is Christ who lives in me." (Gal 2:20 NRSV)

11. Gal 2:19-20 (NRSV).

the darkness that is present with us. This is not what Jesus does. Instead, as Peter reminds us, "When he was abused, he did not return abuse; when he suffered, he did not threaten; but he entrusted himself to the one who judges justly."[12] Jesus doesn't react at all the way we would expect. Instead he bears it all and somehow finds compassion enough to ask for his enemies to be forgiven.

This is the task that each of us is called to—look square at our sin, our shame, and darkness and learn to accept them for what they are. It sounds wrong. It sounds backward. But only by embracing our darkness can it be disarmed. It thrives on resistance, on hatred, on opposition. Frankly, it doesn't know how to handle being loved and embraced. We may not know how to embrace it, but Jesus does. That is why we must learn "to live within the faithfulness of the Son of God," and stop trying to muster up our own.

Eventually we learn to be thankful for our hang-ups, because without them we would never be willing to venture out to a new possibility. We also become thankful for the cross, because through it we learn what it looks like truly to let go. Paul found this gratitude and expressed in Galatians 6:

> "For my part, I am going to boast about nothing but the Cross of our Master, Jesus Christ. Because of that Cross, I have been crucified in relation to the world, set free from the stifling atmosphere of pleasing others and fitting into the little patterns that they dictate. Can't you see the central issue in all this? It is not what you and I do—submit to circumcision, reject circumcision. It is what *God* is doing, and he is creating something totally new, a free life!"[13]

Jesus has shown us who we truly are, and how we can live in that identity. When we face our darkness and realize how much our defense mechanisms and pain numbing strategies are killing us, we begin to let them die off.

Ultimately we experience some kind of death no matter how we look at it. We will either endure the excruciating death that comes from ignoring who we truly are, or we will journey down to the depths to find the life that God is offering us.

12. 1 Pet 2:23 (NRSV).
13. Gal 6:14-16 (MSG).

CHAPTER 13

Removing the Slate

FOR THE LAST SEVERAL years I have worked in technology support for a school district in Northern California. It is probably the best job I've ever had. I get to help people resolve their technology issues and relieve their stress. After all, there's not much worse for a teacher than leading a room full of impatient children and having the computer or projector stop working. When I stroll into their classrooms, I am often hailed as a hero, and sometimes it looks as though I have magical powers.

I cannot tell you how many times I have arrived on the scene to fix an issue and find that the problem resolves itself as soon as I walk in the door. In the moment it feels like a relief, but it can actually be very frustrating. The reason is that it is very difficult for me to identify the underlying issue if I cannot see the symptoms. So sometimes it's a good thing that the browser won't load, the computer shuts down, or the printer jams up, because I then have something to work with in order to discover the issue. Failure to operate becomes a welcome occurrence.

In church circles, we are often overly concerned with and afraid of failure. We focus on behavior modification in order to avoid dealing with God's response. Much of this stems from a cold, judicial understanding of the way God forgives.

This came out pretty clearly one evening when I was in high school. Our church youth group carpooled to a local theater and filed into our seats to take in a skit. I wasn't entirely sure what the theme of the performance was, but I enjoyed being with everyone so much I didn't really care. The voices began to quiet down as the lights dimmed. It soon became clear that the show was meant to be evangelistic, but as is often the case, fear was used as the ultimate motivator.

Two scenarios were presented to the audience. First, four teenagers are cruising around listening to Christian music when they suffer a terrible car accident. Because they were Christians, and because they were honoring God by listening to the right kind of music, they are rewarded with an eternity in heaven.

The second scenario, as you can probably guess, was quite the contrast. In this instance, four teenagers are off for a joyride. There is no explicit explanation indicating whether the teenagers are Christians or not. However, they are listening to secular music, and because of this infraction, they are destined for hell after they perish.

Now there's a lot of disturbing messages going on in this performance, many of which I was blind to in those days. But one in particular is the nature of God's forgiveness. It sees forgiveness as an impersonal transaction. Apparently God holds some pretty impressive grudges, and unless you explicitly ask for forgiveness for all the ways you have sinned, God will continue to hold that grudge for all eternity. I know people who can hold some pretty stubborn grudges, but this is on a whole other level.

Evangelicals value forgiveness, arguably above everything else. Forgiveness is our pathway to eternal life. The problem is that the way we often talk about God and the cross undermines this pivotal value.

We were taught that the purpose of the Old Testament law was to soothe God's anger. We sin, God gets angry, and blood has to be spilled to solve the issue. After all, the writer to the Hebrews tells us, "Without the shedding of blood there is no forgiveness of sins."[1]

Eventually God gets so fed up that he gives up on the Israelites and kicks them out of the promised land. After his temper cools off he paves the way for them to return home, but it's not a permanent fix. God needs something more substantial to satisfy his anger, and to resolve the grudge which he cannot let go.

So with that in mind, God sends his Son. Jesus represents us, and because he lived a perfect life, he is a suitable substitute to be punished in our place. The problem is that in this gospel narrative, God can only bring himself to forgive once a suitable payment has been made. Once payment is made, however, it is no longer forgiveness. As Greg Boyd asks, "If God must always get what's coming to him in order to forgive, does God ever really forgive?"[2] That's one reason this gospel narrative doesn't work.

---

1. Heb 9:22 (NRSV).

2. Beilby and Eddy, *Nature of the Atonement*, 104.

This notion of forgiveness partly stems from us inferring a sense of judicial justice from the Old Testament law, where forgiveness seems only to come after plenty of ritual and pleading. This is a misrepresentation of the purpose of the law, but it also misses a point that Paul makes in Galatians. Paul explained that before the Old Testament law and sacrificial system were put into place, God offered an unconditional promise to Abraham. God promised to bless Abraham, and through him to bless the entire world. That promise is greater than the law that came after it. There is something deeper than ritual and sacrifice. God doesn't need anything from us to be love, he simply is love.

We can see this throughout the Old Testament, interspersed among the tales of violence and retribution. God forgives many times without requiring punishment or seeking vengeance. Hosea is one of the most moving books in scripture, and a great example of this. We can feel the pain coming from God as he watches his people reject him over and over again. There is talk of punishment, of rejection, of giving Israel up. There are remaining elements from the concept of God as an agent of wrath, but there is also genuine relational strife. Finally God pours out his heart,

> "How can I give you up, Ephraim? How can I hand you over, Israel . . . My heart is changed within me; all my compassion is aroused. I will not carry out my fierce anger, nor will I devastate Ephraim again. For I am God, and not a man—the Holy One among you. I will not come against their cities."[3]

God, seemingly against all reason, logic, and expectation, decides to draw Israel back to him. And his reason is monumental: "For I am God, and not a man." It is our nature to payback and hold grudges, but it is God's nature to pardon. As Isaiah pronounced, "Let the wicked forsake their ways and the unrighteous their thoughts. Let them turn to the Lord, and he will have mercy on them, and to our God, for he will freely pardon."[4]

Why does God freely pardon? "For my thoughts are not your thoughts, neither are your ways my ways," declares the Lord. "As the heavens are higher than the earth, so are my ways higher than your ways and my thoughts than your thoughts."[5]

We are the ones who hold grudges, not the Abba of Jesus. So when we make the cross about God requiring payment or punishment in order to forgive, we're projecting our own tendencies. It's important to understand

---

3. Hos 11:8–9 (NIV).

4. Isa 55:7 (NIV).

5. Isa 55:8–9 (NIV).

that God does not need Jesus to die in order to forgive us. God is a forgiving God. He always has been. Brian Zhand puts it, "The crucifixion is not what God inflicts upon Jesus in order to forgive; the crucifixion is what God endures in Christ as he forgives."[6] Or as Paul expressed, "God was reconciling the world to himself in Christ, not counting people's sins against them."[7] Jesus died, not so we can be forgiven, but because God is a forgiving God.

When we frame the cross otherwise, and make it about a punishment or payoff, we are undercutting God's mercy and portraying him as angry and vengeful. When's the last time you felt comfortable confessing a wrongdoing to someone with a vindictive streak? It doesn't work that way. Thus, this way of talking of the cross had me running in the opposite direction.

The cross and forgiveness are, however, intimately linked. Paul speaks of one crucial connection in his letter to the Colossians. "When you were dead in your sins and in the uncircumcision of your flesh, God made you alive with Christ. He forgave us all our sins, having canceled the charge of our legal indebtedness, which stood against us and condemned us; he has taken it away, nailing it to the cross."[8]

According to Paul, Jesus provides forgiveness in a powerful way, not by offering a payment or appeasement to God, but by destroying the very system that requires such things. The very notion of sacrifices and offering payments for guilt, as we looked at earlier, was originally our concept and our design. God worked with us where we were, but through Jesus he does away with the whole notion. Jesus doesn't appease God, but instead undermines the idea that God has to be appeased in the first place. I hoped God would let me off the hook for my screw-ups, but as my spiritual director put it, "God doesn't have a hook."

This message is foundational to the book of Hebrews. Jesus becomes our sacrifice "once for all."[9] As Michael Hardin explains in his book *The Jesus Driven Life*, the author of Hebrews uses sacrificial language to undermine the sacrificial system.[10] When it tells us that there is no forgiveness without the shedding of blood, it's referring to the human system of sacrifice, and Jesus offers himself up in death to undo the whole thing. Sacrifice is the problem, and Jesus submits himself to it in order to undo it. As Mark Heim reinforces concerning Hebrews, "What we have here is a capsule summary of the nature of sacrificial violence, presented as exactly what Jesus's

6. Zhand, *Sinners in the Hands*, 89-90.

7. 2 Cor 5:19 (NIV).

8. Col 2:13-14 (NIV).

9. Heb 10:10 (NIV).

10. Hardin, *Jesus Driven Life*, 7646.

death is not about. Christ's sacrifice is presented as the opposite and in fact the end of that dynamic. His sacrifice was meant to stop it."[11]

Our concept of forgiveness has often been linked with the common belief that salvation is merely about going to heaven when we die, along with the idea that holiness or righteousness is a legal concept. So God's forgiveness became a way to make us legally innocent in order to be eligible for paradise. It makes forgiveness very impersonal, and doesn't impact us here and now in our shame.

God makes it much more personal than that. It's not about a legal standing; it was never about that. Don't get me wrong, knowing we have a "clean slate" is beautiful, but the cross is showing us that there was never a slate to begin with. It is showing us the real purpose behind genuine and heartfelt forgiveness: reconciliation. God doesn't just want to forgive, he wants to show us how to live in the forgiveness he always offers.

That's why, as Paul speaks of in Philippians 2, God lowers or empties himself. It's so painful and difficult to continue in a relationship where there has been hurt and forgiveness offered. It's the only way, but it's excruciating. It will not work if the one offering forgiveness has an attitude of moral superiority, or even pity. There has to be an even playing field, and an understanding that though I have been hurt and treated poorly, I am no better. I have just as much capacity to be manipulative and selfish.

To this end God does something truly astonishing. He lowers himself as much as possible to be on our playing field. While we can't say that he falls into the same tendencies that we do, he does face the same temptations. He is tempted to manipulate, coerce, and oppress just as we are. Amazingly, though he never falls into sin, he is able to make "sinners" perfectly comfortable around him. They even actively seek him out. He holds no grudges and makes no condemnations. Instead, because he has faced the same challenges we do, he can "empathize with our weaknesses."[12]

For a long time forgiveness was a misunderstood concept for me. I was so afraid of God that I determined the easiest way to deal with forgiveness was never to screw up in the first place. When you're just focused on following the rules and looking the part to others, it's not all that challenging. Just ask Paul: "as to the law, a Pharisee; as to zeal, a persecutor of the church; as to righteousness under the law, blameless."[13] Other times, though, when I was drowning in shame, I would constantly ask for forgiveness very anxiously, for anything I had done, or anything I couldn't remember. We have

11. Heim, *Saved From Sacrifice*, 158.
12. Heb 4:15 (NIV).
13. Phil 3:5-6 (NRSV).

to cover our bases when we believe we're dealing with a tyrant. Needless to say, I didn't have much working knowledge of relationship strife and true heart-level forgiveness for a long time.

Things get real very quickly when one gets married. It's one thing if we said an unkind word to a coworker or stranger; it's completely different when the person we hurt is lying in bed next to us. It's an intimate reminder of the unsightly tendencies inside of us, and that they can wreak real havoc on people we care about. It is in those times that I'm grateful to have a wife who doesn't hold my worst moments against me, and doesn't pretend that she's better than I am. I know that when little things remind us of the past, it can be extremely difficult to forgive. Yet she continues to love me.

That's part of what the cross is showing us: forgiveness is brutal. Forgiveness involves death, not the death of the offender as punishment, but the death of the ego in the person who was hurt. The ego wants vindication. The ego demands that someone pay for what was done. The ego tells us the storyline that we are better than those who wronged us, and that we would never stoop to their level.

Forgiveness never works from this mindset, which is why forgiveness is so painful. The process of forgiveness is a mutual humiliation: the offenders are humiliated by the evidence of their own selfishness, and those forgiving willfully humiliate themselves by giving up the illusion of their ego, their moral superiority, and their right for revenge.

This is what God does for us on the cross. He allows himself to be publicly humiliated in order to bring reconciliation. And when Jesus encounters the disciples again—the very ones who fled, abandoned, and denied him—Jesus's word to them is "peace." He gives up his right to get even. As Richard Rhor beautifully words it, "Every time God forgives us, God is saying that God's own rules do not matter as much as the relationship that God wants to create with us."[14]

So many times in my life I have shuddered at the thought of approaching God after I screwed up. I was sure that this was the last straw, the time God would finally have had enough of my weakness. If God forgives by beating his own Son, surely he's going to get fed up with me at some point.

But God forgives us even before Jesus takes his first steps toward the cross. God always forgives. While it's freeing, and therefore important to confess our blindness, our stubbornness, and selfishness to God, we do so not in an attempt to convince him to relent his anger, but instead as a reminder that through thick and thin, right and wrong, God's loving posture

14. Rhor, *Falling Upward*, 56.

toward us never wavers. The pain we endure is self-inflicted. We were, as Paul writes, enemies in our minds.[15]

The God we create in our minds is not the Father of Jesus. His is the Father of the prodigal son. This is the Papa who sees his self-centered, hurtful boy coming home and runs to meet him—not to enact revenge—but to offer his embrace. The Father never changes, and when we dare to trust in this reality, we are transformed.

Ultimately forgiveness is about hope. Hope that a marriage on the rocks can come out on the other side better than ever. Hope that words expressed by a father in stress and anger don't have to result in a life of estrangement and bitterness. Hope that a little boy who once believed he was wretched and no good can one day come to see himself as his Abba does. That's the hope of the cross.

15. Col 1:21 (NIV).

PART IV

YOU'RE NOT WHO I THOUGHT YOU WERE

CHAPTER 14

A Father's Justice

IMAGINE A MAN IN his late 40's named Daniel receives a dreaded phone call one evening.

"Hello sir, are you the father of a Nathaniel Davis?" a serious voice inquires.

"Um, yes. Who wants to know?"

"Sir, this is Officer Reed. I'm sorry to inform you that earlier tonight we found your son on the side of a road badly beaten. He is alive, but unconscious."

Daniel's heart is racing. The phone trembles in his hand as he continues to talk to the officer to find out more details, including where his son is being taken, so he can see him. A million thoughts are racing through his head. What would you be thinking if it were you? Perhaps you've had to suffer through a similar scenario. I imagine I would be focused on praying for my son to recover and wake up soon so I could know he would be okay. I would be wondering how I would break the news to my wife. But among all those thoughts, I imagine at some point I would contemplate how much I wanted the police to catch whoever was responsible for the terrible act. I would want the perpetrator to be sent to prison for years and years and made to suffer for what he had inflicted on my son.

A couple days pass. Daniel and his wife stick close to Nathaniel's bedside, anxiously awaiting his eyes to creak open. Out of the corner of his own eye, Daniel notices Officer Reed approaching the room, appearing to have some unpleasant news.

"Mr. Davis," the officer greets him, extending his hand.

"Yes officer, forgive me, but you look like you have unpleasant news."

"Mr. Davis, do you have another son named Brad?"

"Yes I do. Oh no! Did something happen to him too?"

Officer Reed takes a second to muster up the strength to fill Daniel in.

"Mr. Davis, it appears that your son Brad is the perpetrator. He is the one who did this to Nathaniel."

That would change things, wouldn't it? Before, a father's mindset would have been to make the offender suffer for what he had done. But what if both parties were your children? I would imagine that for most of us we would want restoration and reconciliation for our sons. Though we would be very angry and upset that one of our sons would do such a thing, our ultimate goal would be healing and reconciliation for everyone involved. Simply punishing the wrongdoer doesn't go far enough anymore.

This is the dilemma for Jesus's Abba. In his case, however, he doesn't have just two sons. No, he has billions of children, and they keep on hurting each other. Because they are all his, he cannot be satisfied with simply punishing or even removing those who are doing the hurting. As a good Father, he hopes and seeks for the restoration and reconciliation of all his offspring.

The problem is we sometimes don't speak of God having such natural paternal aspirations. We spoke of forgiveness in the last chapter. Forgiveness sometimes makes us uncomfortable. To us it can seem to undermine justice, and by justice, we usually mean the punishment and suffering of one who has done wrong. We regularly portray God as holding to this notion of justice as well. We often speak and sing of God's anger being appeased when Jesus was punished in our place. We looked at earlier what "wrath of God" really means. In this context, however, we typically are asserting that God was angry at sin and was finally content when sin was violently punished in Jesus. Apparently God considers the case closed once someone gets bludgeoned.

Many Christians would proclaim that there is good news in all of this. If we accept what Jesus has endured on our behalf, we are welcomed into his company. If, however, one were to reject this message, then the punishment that Jesus endured for him is back on the table, only this time, many Christians believe, it will last eternally. Once again, God would be satisfied if people reject him as long as they will be punished for their travesty. The bottom line in this message is that justice is upheld.

Let's put it as plainly as possible and really grasp the significance. In the gospel narrative that many Christians proclaim, God is satisfied if billions of people are separated from him eternally. God is okay with this, because justice has been served. When God cares first and foremost about appeasing his anger toward sin, this is an acceptable outcome. God is content so long as people pay for what they have done. While most Christians would not put it quite this way, it is the logical conclusion if a retributive brand of justice is seen as the ultimate goal, and seen as an essential part of God's character.

When Paul wrote to the Colossians, he gave different criteria for what God seeks:

> "Through (Christ) God was pleased to reconcile to himself all things, whether on earth or in heaven, by making peace through the blood of his cross."[1]

For many Christians, an important part of their faith is the belief that eventually a large portion of humanity will end up suffering eternally in hell. It's not that we want this to happen, it's just that this is the only possible outcome that has been presented to many of us. There are numerous passages, however, that give a glimpse of an alternate ending that has already begun taking place in Christ's work. This is one of those glimpses. Paul claims that in Christ all things were reconciled. The all that Paul refers to here is the same all that, a few verses before, he speaks of being created through Christ, so everyone is included here. In this passage, Paul is saying "all" that was created through Christ is reconciled through him as well. This isn't the only time we read such a message. There are more than a few instances where the New Testament alludes to God bringing all to himself, or at least his desire to do so. Here are some other instances:

> "And I, when I am lifted up from the earth, will draw all people to myself."[2]

> "Therefore God also highly exalted him and gave him the name that is above every name, so that at the name of Jesus every knee should bend, in heaven and on earth and under the earth, and every tongue should confess that Jesus Christ is Lord, to the glory of God the Father."[3]

> "Therefore just as one man's trespass led to condemnation for all, so one man's act of righteousness leads to justification and life for all. For just as by the one man's disobedience the many were made sinners, so by the one man's obedience the many will be made righteous."[4]

---

1. Col 1:20 (NRSV).
2. John 12:32 (NRSV).
3. Phil 2:9-11 (NRSV).
4. Rom 5:18-19 (NRSV).

"For God has imprisoned all in disobedience so that he may be merciful to all."[5]

"(God) who wants all people to be saved and to come to a knowledge of the truth. For there is one God and one mediator between God and mankind, the man Christ Jesus, who gave himself as a ransom for all people."[6]

"The Lord is not slow about his promise, as some think of slowness, but is patient with you, not wanting any to perish, but all to come to repentance."[7]

"My little children, I am writing these things to you so that you may not sin. But if anyone does sin, we have an advocate with the Father, Jesus Christ the righteous; and he is the atoning sacrifice for our sins, and not for ours only but also for the sins of the whole world."[8]

At this point, someone may ask, "Doesn't God speak of judgement and give warnings to those that follow their own way?" Yes, and we'll look at those more closely later. The problem is that, in many of my church environments, we assumed that all references to judgement were about anger and punishment, and then we pretended that the passages listed here didn't even exist. The reality is that if people were to read these passages by themselves without any knowledge of the rest of scripture, they would most likely assume that God's salvation will come to everyone. We at least need to wrestle with that.

While the spectrum of salvation is nothing any of us can know for sure, we can at minimum infer from these passages that God's desire is for salvation to come to all humanity. That's important.

We stumble over this because we want justice. We think of all the people who have hurt others. Maybe we think of someone who cheated or betrayed us. We want to know when they are going to pay for their wrongs. There are rapists, murderers, and slave traders running amuck all over the world. We've been around the block enough to know that many of them will not be captured or forced to answer for their crimes in this lifetime, so we hope for justice to be done in the next. This usually takes the form of eternal hell.

5. Rom 11:32 (NRSV).

6. 1 Tim 2:4-6 (NIV).

7. 2 Pet 3:9 (NRSV).

8. 1 John 2:1-2 (NRSV).

If we believe that some people must end up there, the question becomes: where is the line drawn? What actions should land one in hell? Many who hold to this belief would say anyone who murders should face hell as a consequence. Others would draw the line in a different location and include anyone who has molested a child. In other parts of the world people would be condemned for different criteria, such as for committing adultery or being gay. It turns out to be more convoluted than we like to imagine. (And if turning to Jesus rectifies all of this, why would God take that option off the table after death? More on that later).

Most of the time our criteria for who should be condemned turns out to be pretty self-involved. We want this person to pay because she hurt me. We want this other person to face punishment because he violated the principles that make sense to me. This is so profoundly shown in *The Shack* in a conversation between the main character, Mack, and Sarayu—the Holy Spirit. Sarayu inquires,

> "When something happens to you, how do you determine whether it is good or evil?"
>
> Mack thought for a moment before answering. "Well, I haven't really thought about that. I guess I would say that something is good when I like it-when it makes me feel good or gives me a sense of security. Conversely, I'd call something evil that causes me pain or costs me something I want."
>
> "So it is pretty subjective then?"
>
> "I guess it is."
>
> "And how confident are you in your ability to discern what indeed is good for you, or what is evil?"
>
> "To be honest," said Mack, "I tend to sound justifiably angry when somebody is threatening my 'good,' you know, what I think I deserve. But I'm not really sure I have any logical ground for deciding what is actually good or evil, except how something or someone affects me . . . All seems quite self-serving and self-centered, I suppose."[9]

We filter our sense of good and evil, and in turn our sense of justice, through our own self-preservation. We are often ready to cast people aside until it involves someone we value. We want the one who victimized our child to be written off until we find out that perpetrator is our other child. For God, they're all his children.

A decent parent in that situation would long for more than punishment or retribution. He would pray endlessly that the beaten son would

9. Young, *Shack*, 134.

wake up and fully recover. At the same time he would pray that, in the midst of facing the consequences for his actions, the other son would confess and repent. He would hope desperately that someday the family would be whole again. The absence of either son would render the family incomplete.

A decent father or mother would react this way, but God is better than decent. As Jesus reasoned when addressing prayer, "If you then, who are evil, know how to give good gifts to your children, how much more will your Father in heaven give good things to those who ask him!"[10] God is a good Father. When any parent is facing the wrongdoing of a child or loved one, tit for tat justice goes out the window. We want redemption.

This is why the Father Jesus speaks of is so gracious. Our tendency is to give little interest to people who don't look like us or advance our agenda. If they negatively impact us, our inclination is to return the favor. The Father, on the other hand, "Makes his sun rise on the evil and on the good, and sends rain on the righteous and on the unrighteous."[11] He hires someone for one hour of work and gives them a full day's pay. He invites anyone who will have him to come to his banquets, whether good or bad, prominent or lowly. God is gracious regardless of whether we appear to deserve it or not.

This is one of the reasons the religious elite had such a problem with Jesus. They simply didn't understand by what system he was operating. They had crafted such impressive resumes; yet, Jesus didn't seem to care. It was why those who were aware of their moral failures and the downtrodden were so drawn to him. They already knew that they didn't deserve anything, and here was a prophet and a rabbi who didn't seem to care about that either.

Jesus didn't exclude anyone. He did, however, fiercely oppose the way religious leaders would oppress others and distort his Father's grace. But the invitation to repent was always there. He wept over the city that would eventually execute him. He used his last breaths to cry out for the forgiveness of his enemies.

Jesus doesn't exclude, but we typically do. Once again, our categorizing process is completely based on our limited understanding. We ostracize others because they don't look like us, sound like us, think like us, or act like us.

We, of course, convince ourselves that it's all for a higher purpose. We claim that we don't want to enable others or encourage bad behaviors. Now, there are times where we must set up healthy boundaries to keep people safe. Most of the time, however, we exclude simply because people don't fit our expectations.

10. Matt 7:11 (NRSV).

11. Matt 5:45 (NRSV).

In my experience, this is about as common among us Christians as it is among anyone else. The Church can be a place where those who know they are broken can gratefully share the belief that there is a compassionate God who doesn't use our weaknesses and hang-ups against us. Unfortunately, Christian communities sometimes forsake this purpose. People are outcast for their struggles instead of finding a safe place.

The exclusion doesn't just apply to others. When we live this way, we tend to banish and condemn the more unsightly parts of ourselves. Deep down we know that we can be selfish, manipulative, and hurtful. The only way our egos know how to deal with these realities is through self-loathing or self-promotion. Either way, we try to hide and ignore our shadow.

Here's the problem: the only way we find healing and freedom is by facing our shadow and our skeletons. We face them and accept them for what they are. When we finally see the darkness in us and experience love even in the depths, that's when healing really begins.

We will find this difficult to do, however, if we understand God's justice to be about retribution and excluding that which is unworthy. If God can be satisfied with casting off many of his children, then it behooves us to live in fear and dread. This is what has fueled much of my anxiety.

But this is not the Abba that Jesus speaks of, nor is this his desire for his children. God waits patiently for us to awaken from our stubborn delusions and come home. He wants that for each one of us. Our Abba could not be pleased with anything less.

CHAPTER 15

Redeemable Quality

HIDE AND SEEK NEVER gets old. I remember playing with my mom when I was little. On Sundays after church I would run, hide, and wait to be found. Even when she found me I would wait to give myself up, believing that she could not see me if I couldn't see her. In high school my friends and I would play outside at night, with the darkness providing loads of suspense. Now I play with our son at the park, or even with our dogs. They're excellent seekers; the hiding part is sort of lost on them though.

People are generally pretty good at hiding, not just during games, but in many areas of our lives. Actually, we're a little too good. Humanity started hiding in the beginning when Adam and Eve ran away from God. They hid from him, and covered themselves to hide from each other. I followed suit when I was wrestling with my addiction to pornography. I could have found help and healing by opening up to people I trusted. (Of course, this is not very easy in certain religious environments, but that's another issue). Instead, I thought I could make things better by hiding and stuffing everything down. We often try to fix things and end up making them worse.

This is one of the impacts of the way we often portray the Gospel. In our telling of it we portray Jesus as coming to save us from the Father. In reality, he arrives on the scene to save us from ourselves.

Jesus communicates this in the quintessential Gospel passage:

> "For God so loved the world that he gave his one and only Son, that whoever believes in him shall not perish but have eternal life. For God did not send his Son into the world to condemn the world, but to save the world through him. Whoever believes in him is not condemned, but whoever does not believe stands

condemned already because they have not believed in the name
of God's one and only Son."[1]

Jesus is saying that anyone who believes in him will experience eternal life.
This term "eternal life" used in the Gospel of John is synonymous with the
term "kingdom of God" in the other Gospels. The kingdom of God is not a
future only reality but instead begins now. The same applies to eternal life.
Thus Jesus prays, "Now this is eternal life: that they know you, the only true
God, and Jesus Christ, whom you have sent."[2]

Eternal life is knowing a benevolent God who has united himself with
us and will never give up on us. It is seeing the Son and knowing that he
reflects our true identity. Living outside of this reality, as we talked about
before, is the essence of sin. It is living a life that leads to a self-loathing, condemning, and empty existence. That's why Jesus says that those who don't
believe in this love are already condemning themselves.

So this passage is not saying that God is going to punish and condemn
those who don't follow his way. It would be odd, wouldn't it, for Jesus to say,
"God did not send his Son to condemn the world, but if you don't believe . . .
he's going to condemn you." That is the summation of the Gospel for many
Christians, though. It's the message that tormented me for many years.

So why does Jesus seemingly speak of hell, or torment, or gnashing of
teeth so much? Isn't he speaking of an afterlife of torture or punishment for
those who don't obey God?

Jesus used a particular word that was understood by many of his con-
temporaries in this way. That word was *Gehenna*, and it's the word we translate as hell. This word originally derived from a valley outside of Jerusalem
called the Valley of the Sons of Hinnom. This valley became infamous. It
was the site where Israelites would sacrifice their children to the foreign
god, Molech. Eventually one of Israel's kings, Josiah, would take it upon
himself to reform the people's ways. He destroyed all of the altars and idols
associated with Israel's disobedience.

Israel continued to reject their calling to be a light to the nations and
instead mimicked all the powers around them. In turn, Israel was conquered
and exiled, and Judah followed them. Jerusalem was conquered, burned, and
the resulting bodies were thrown in the Valley that would come to be known
as *Gehenna*. This valley became a "metaphor for historic destruction."[3]

Over time this metaphor transformed from a picture of historic destruction to a pointer toward torment in the afterlife. What this torment

1. John 3:16-18 (NIV).
2. John 17:3 (NIV).
3. Jersak, *Her Gates*, 43.

looked like, as well as the duration, differed. Some viewed the torment as leading to annihilation. Others viewed it as torment over a period of time, after which people would be destroyed or restored. Still others viewed it as ongoing torment. This developed between the time of the exile and the time of Jesus in some of the Apocryphal literature, as well as among the Talmudic rabbis. Thus, as Gregory McDonald explains, "The concept of Gehenna in Second Temple literature was evocative and commonly employed but was highly ambiguous and somewhat flexible."[4]

The bottom line, however, was that *Gehenna* became a metaphor for hell in the afterlife. This was a common view around Jesus time. It would be natural to assume that Jesus held this view unless he made a point to differentiate the way he used the word, as some have argued. But as Brad Jersak demonstrates in his book *Her Gates Will Never Be Shut,* Jesus points to a different understanding of *Gehenna* in the way that he aligns himself with the ministry of Jeremiah.

For the prophet Jeremiah, *Gehenna,* or the Valley of Hinnom, was not referring to eternal torment but to real life consequences for our sin. Jeremiah was one who condemned the sin that was taking place in this valley, warned of the coming destruction of Jerusalem, and foretold the transformation of the valley into a mass grave. What we find in the Gospels is that Jesus closely aligns himself with Jeremiah in his ministry, as well as with Jeremiah's view of *Gehenna.*[5] As Jersak elaborates, "For Jesus, Gehenna referred primarily to the self-destructive consequences of rebellion . . . Gehenna is judgment to be sure—and may even point secondarily to final judgment—but the picture is first of all about the destructive wake left behind by our sin here and now, not an afterlife of eternal, conscious torment. It is quite literally "the way of death."[6]

---

4. McDonald, *Evangelical Universalist,* 144.

5. As Jersak details, "Jesus identified himself strongly with the ministry of Jeremiah, especially through his Passion Week. With his symbolic enactment of the overthrow of the temple, he was consciously recapitulating the oracle of Jeremiah 7. In his famous "den of thieves" reference, Jesus quoted Jeremiah to deconstruct the security of the temple establishment (Jer 7: 11 = Matt 21: 13/ Mark 11: 17/ Luke 19: 46; see also Isa 56: 7 = Mark 11: 17). His woes in Matt 23 to the scribes and teachers of the law no doubt echoed Jer 8: 8 ("the false pen of the Scribes") and Jer 23: 1 ("Woe to the shepherds who are destroying and scattering the sheep of my pasture!"). When Jesus cursed the fig tree's fruitlessness and it withered (Matt 21; Mark 11), he seemed to be drawing from Jer 8: 13: "I will take away their harvest, declares the LORD. . . . There will be no figs on the tree, and their leaves will wither. What I have given them will be taken from them." Finally, that same week, Jesus consciously activated the New Covenant as a prophetic fulfillment of Jer 31–33 (esp. 31: 31) with the Passover Cup (Luke 22: 20)." (*Her Gates,* 57)

6. Ibid, 60–61.

Even that, however, is not the end. Jeremiah, whom Jesus very much seems to be referencing in his speaking of *Gehenna*, offers a New Covenant promise to his people from God. This is the promise Jesus references on the night before his crucifixion. What's incredible about this New Covenant reference is that the valley, from which the metaphor of *Gehenna* would derive, is included in God's restoration plan. Jeremiah 31: 38-40 reads,

> "The days are coming," declares the Lord, "when this city will be rebuilt for me from the Tower of Hananel to the Corner Gate. The measuring line will stretch from there straight to the hill of Gareb and then turn to Goah. The whole valley where dead bodies and ashes are thrown, and all the terraces out to the Kidron Valley on the east as far as the corner of the Horse Gate, will be holy to the Lord. The city will never again be uprooted or demolished."[7]

The valley, which would come to be the metaphor for destruction when we seek our own way, is said to be restored to be "holy to the Lord." Let me say that again: The valley of *Gehenna*, which becomes known to some as an indicator of eternal punishment, is said to be transformed and restored by God. That sends chills down my spine. That should make us think twice about ever questioning the mercy and transforming drive in the heart of God. Apparently no matter how far gone we are, God is not willing to give up.

Jesus also speaks of *Gehenna* as the experience of being lost or separated from God. That's because heaven and hell are not about a time and place where something eventually happens. Jesus said that the kingdom of God is near, within us. Eternal life is knowing the Father and the Son now. In the same way, *Gehenna* is about experiencing life without that now. As my spiritual director once put it, "Heaven and hell are relational realities, not linear realities." This echoes St. Isaac of Ninevah, who asserted that "Hell is an "effect," not a "substance," while the "outer darkness" is not a place but "the state without any delight in true knowledge and communion with God."[8]

So when Jesus says, "It is easier for a camel to go through the eye of a needle than for someone who is rich to enter the kingdom of God,"[9] or when Paul lays out a list of selfish and sinful acts people can fall into and says, "I am warning you, as I warned you before: those who do such things will not

---

7. Jer 31:38-40 (NIV).

8. Ware, "Dare We Hope," para. 44.

9. Mark 10:25 (NIV).

inherit the kingdom of God,"[10] they're not talking about getting kicked out of heaven. They are saying that heaven is an ever-present reality. If we want to experience it, Christ shows us the way.

Heaven and hell become two ways of experiencing reality around us. This comes through subtly in the story of the rich man and Lazarus. They are both in Hades after they die, but Lazarus is with Abraham while the rich man suffers miserably. The rich man still wants Lazarus to serve him. "He doesn't deign to speak with Lazarus directly but addresses himself only to Abraham. He still views Lazarus as an inferior being, thought of, if at all, as the help."[11] The rich man suffers from his distorted view of reality.

Often Christians will point to this parable as an example of eternal punishment for those who do not honor God with their lives. They see the chasm between the rich man and Lazarus as a physical chasm between heaven and hell that no one can cross. As Abraham says in the story, "Those who might want to pass from here to you cannot do so, and no one can cross from there to us."[12] What we forget is that this is the very chasm Jesus crossed when he descended into hell, as we confess in our creeds. It may have been impassable at one time, but now Jesus has conquered.

Another time in a common passage that seems to support many Christians's view of hell and judgment is when Jesus separates people based on their service to the less fortunate. The parable refers to those who remembered the less fortunate as sheep, and those who did not as goats. "All the nations will be gathered before him, and he will separate people one from another as a shepherd separates the sheep from the goats, and he will put the sheep at his right hand and the goats at the left."[13] The sheep are said to go off to eternal life, while the goats are off to eternal punishment.

There's a couple of things that we need to remember when approaching passages such as this one. First, it's important to recognize that, among other things, Jesus is a prophet. Prophets tend to explain things in unorthodox and hyperbolic ways to get a point across. For example, Jesus told people that if they were prone to lusting with their eyes, they could simply tear their eyes out to solve the problem. In another instance, he expressed that no one could be his disciple unless they hated their family members.

Secondly, when we hear the phrase "eternal punishment," we assume that this describes retributive punishment that lasts eternally. This is just one way to interpret this phrase. The word for eternal doesn't always mean

---

10. Gal 5:21 (NRSV).

11. Zhand, *Sinners in the Hands*, 133.

12. Luke 16:26 (NRSV).

13. Matt 25:32-33 (NRSV).

literally forever. For example, the same word is used in the Greek Old Testament when describing how long Jonah was in the whale. Another example is Jude's reference to Sodom and Gomorrah being punished by eternal fire. Sometimes eternal can refer to the duration of the effects of God's actions rather than the actions themselves.

This could be describing, therefore, a punishment that has a redirecting purpose with eternal results. Frankly, a punishment that literally lasts all eternity could only provide satisfaction to a sadistic deity. That's not the God we're dealing with, however, because even in the Old Testament he is recognized as being "slow to anger."[14] Kallistos Ware puts it this way: "If the aim of punishment is to heal, then once the healing has been accomplished there is no need for the punishment to continue. If, however, the punishment is supposed to be everlasting, it is difficult to see how it can have any remedial or educative purpose. In a never-ending hell there is no escape and therefore no healing, and so the infliction of punishment in such a hell is pointless and immoral."[15] This was, however, the image of God I had in my head for years. There's simply no winning with that type of torturous entity.

Of course, this is not the main point of these parables anyway. Jesus speaks to people who often view others as the rich man viewed Lazarus and who often ignore their pain and plight. The point is to repent, to experience life now. Otherwise we risk facing *Gehenna* now—one designed by the consequences of our selfishness and condemnation.

The last thing Jesus would be communicating is that God will be vindictively punishing people for all eternity by torturing them with fire. How could we believe that when Jesus tells us to love our enemies so "that you may be children of your Father in heaven"?[16] How could we believe God would act in such a way when, while he is being crucified, Jesus displayed God's character by praying, "Father forgive them; for they do not know what they are doing"?[17]

But God is a consuming fire, and often his presence can be painful, not because he seeks to inflict pain, but because he seeks to heal. After all, healing can be a painful experience. Paul alludes to this when he describes our life's work being tested by fire: "On the judgment day, fire will reveal what kind of work each builder has done. The fire will show if a person's work has any value. If the work survives, that builder will receive a reward.

14. Ps 103:8 (NIV).
15. Ware, "Dare We Hope," para. 38.
16. Matt 5:45 (NRSV).
17. Luke 23:24 (NRSV).

But if the work is burned up, the builder will suffer great loss. The builder will be saved, but like someone barely escaping through a wall of flames."[18]

God is a consuming fire, not a condemning one. He continually gives us space to become more the people we were made to be. We are the ones who judge, condemn, and shun. We often do this most severely to ourselves. When we see the selfish and manipulative parts of ourselves, we tend to cover them up and pretend they don't exist. This results in intense self-loathing, ignorant arrogance, or both.

Over time this transforms our sense of identity, when we can scarcely believe there is anything truly beautiful inside of us. We try to take the situation into our own hands and end up being our own worst enemy. We condemn the dark parts of ourselves to avoid hell, but we discover that, by living in self-hatred and isolation, we design hell all around us.

This was my life. I can be ruthless to myself. I know exactly how to hurt myself deepest, and when I lose sight of God's love for me, I will tear myself apart. The fires of *Gehenna* have long burned inside my soul.

For all practical purposes I had given up on myself. I just figured this was the way it was always going to be. There was a pit inside me that would never let me enjoy anything. I remember even moments of pleasure and laughter would make me sad because, just as soon as I would begin to enjoy myself, the pit would bring me back. I thank God for the people he's placed in my life who would not allow me to stay there. They have helped me see, as Kallistos Ware expresses, "The creation in its entirety is God's handiwork; in their inner essence all created things are "exceedingly good."[19] This is the truth of who we are.

One Sunday I decided to visit an Eastern Catholic church. It was simultaneously one of the most awkward and moving experiences of my life. I felt uncomfortable and out of place; yet, inexplicable tears kept flowing. There were icons all around. Some sat on stands while others peppered the walls.

As we finished the liturgy and began exiting, an icon caught my eye. I had seen the icon of the resurrection before on the internet or in books, but never up close. It was breathtaking. If you're unfamiliar with the icon, it's probably not what you'd expect. There is no tomb or stone rolled away. In fact, it depicts the day before the resurrection.

On that day Jesus is said to have "descended into hell." In the icon, the gates of hell have been broken, and in each hand Jesus is lifting Adam and

18. 1 Cor 3:13-15 (NIV).
19. Ware, *Orthodox Way,* 743.

Eve up from the depths. The two represent humanity being rescued by Jesus. After all, hell is not a linear reality, it is a relational one.

Adam and Eve are said to be the original people created in God's image, and represent all of us. Thus, because of Jesus's incarnation, we are all united to God at an even deeper level. There is something true about us that trumps the lies, failures, and scars we have endured.

Hell is the false reality we live in. It's what happens when we come to the conclusion that there is nothing left in us that is good, worthy, or pure. But Jesus descends into our *Gehenna*, because no matter what we believe about ourselves, there is a redeemable quality in each one of us. It is God with us and in us.

I don't need Jesus to save me from hell someday. He's already saved me from hell, because when I thought there was nothing worthwhile in me, he showed me otherwise. That's why I love him.

CHAPTER 16

His Mercy Never Ends

I THINK I WAS eleven or twelve at the time. I was attending a church camp, and it was time for the evening chapel service. The service began as the other ones had, with singing and worship. The theme of that night was understanding the magnitude of facing judgment at the end.

It was well timed for me as I was approaching the age of accountability. If you're not familiar with that concept, it is the belief that children under a certain age (often twelve) are automatically saved if they were to die because they did not have the faculties to make an informed decision for or against Christ. Those over that age are said to be accountable for their decision.

Apparently the leaders of the camp did not think a simple sermon would convey the magnitude of fear and torment that could accost someone at the end, so they put us through an intense experience. My memory is a little fuzzy, but I recall certain pieces. I remember there was frightening music playing. The camp volunteers suddenly transformed into bearers of judgement. One image, however, was burned into my mind.

There was one camp volunteer who was incredibly popular with us kids. He was a pastor in our area and was basically a big, fun loving teddy bear. He was someone we knew we could approach with comfort and ease.

That night in chapel, however, he was presented to us as the image of divine judgment. Some of us were chosen for heaven, some for hell, and his large, intimidating finger was the indication of our destination. Above all, though, I remember his face. It communicated anger, hate, and fear. It was difficult to look at him again as I used to.

The whole thing was confusing, though at the time I could not have explained why. We had started the service by singing worship songs about how God is good, and loving, and kind. We read in scripture that God's mercy endures forever; his anger lasts only for a moment. But now we were learning that God was also the main character in our nightmares. If they were trying to convey what many Christians believe about the end times, they could not have done a better job. Someday, many believe, God will give up the nice guy act and let his true colors shine.

I don't mean to convey that those camp leaders and volunteers were mean people who tried to make kids toss and turn at night. This was simply what we had been taught. It was also communicated in the play I mentioned with the two groups of teens crashing in their cars. Even if people want to change their mind, even if they are brought to a new realization that they could not see before, God will say, "You're too late."

One of the reasons this concept has bothered me so much is that it just doesn't add up with what we proclaim about the Gospel. We are told that God went to unspeakable lengths in order to rescue us. He sent his Son knowing that the result would be death at the hands of those who scape-goated him. Jesus voluntarily is said to have lowered himself to be with us. Eugene Peterson phrases that iconic passage from Philippians 2 this way:

> "He had equal status with God but didn't think so much of him-self that he had to cling to the advantages of that status no matter what. Not at all. When the time came, he set aside the privi-leges of deity and took on the status of a slave, became *human*! Having become human, he stayed human. It was an incredibly humbling process. He didn't claim special privileges. Instead, he lived a selfless, obedient life and then died a selfless, obedient death—and the worst kind of death at that—a crucifixion."[1]

God stopped at nothing to draw us to himself. Why would he go to such lengths and yet deny himself his deepest desire because we didn't make the cut off? In college some of the professors would lock the doors to the class-room on test day if a student did not make it on time. It's a tough way to teach kids responsibility. I get that. But what if a terrible storm was coming, like a tornado or a hurricane, and the kids did not arrive at the appointed time? Would we say, "We're sorry, but we gave you fair warning. You'll have to fend for yourself"? I would hope not. It sounds cruel because it is cruel. As we saw before, God's corrections and disciplines are to lead us in the right direction, not to offer a death verdict.

What is it about death that allows it to have a say in our ability to choose God? Granted, there are places in scripture that hint at this, almost

---

1. Phil 2:5-8 (MSG).

in passing. Often they are hyperbolic elements in Jesus's parables to lead people toward a choice now.

One of the verses that has always come to mind on this idea is Hebrews 9:27, "It is appointed for mortals to die once, and after that the judgment."[2] We tend to assume that refers to a condemnation that comes from God, but as we've seen, we are the condemning ones, not God. In fact, the word used here for judgment is the word from which we get "crisis." It is when we are faced with truth, with nowhere to hide. We are forced to make a choice, because the danger of *Gehenna* is a present reality. Kallistos Ware elaborates,

> "The Last Judgement is best understood as the moment of truth when everything is brought to light, when all our acts of choice stand revealed to us in their full implications, when we realize with absolute clarity who we are and what has been the deep meaning and aim of our life. And so, following this final clarification, we shall enter—with soul and body reunited—into heaven or hell, into eternal life or eternal death. Christ is the judge; and yet, from another point of view, it is we who pronounce judgement upon ourselves. If anyone is in hell, it is not because God has imprisoned him there, but because that is where he himself has chosen to be. The lost in hell are self-condemned, self-enslaved; it has been rightly said that the doors of hell are locked on the inside."[3]

Additionally, the next verse continues, "So Christ, having been offered once to bear the sins of many, will appear a second time, not to deal with sin, but to save those who are eagerly waiting for him."[4] The judgment that we bear is a self-inflicted one; and yet, on the cross Jesus endured the effects of our sin. He bears them so he can show us the way through. This is not a passage about God inflicting suffering on us, but about Jesus working to rescue us. Those who are not eagerly waiting for him are not violently punished, because that would be out of God's character. Instead, they endure their own self-inflicted pain from refusing love.

One day after class I decided to ask my professor at seminary about this. I was somewhat timid, fearing that my inquiry might be out of bounds. So somewhat hesitantly I presented my concern. "Why would God go to all this trouble but then turn people away because death is some kind of cutoff point?" His response was simple and brief, yet incredibly profound.

"That doesn't seem to view the resurrection very highly, does it?"

---

2. Heb 9:27 (NRSV).

3. Ware, *Orthodox Way*, 2466.

4. Heb 9:28 (NRSV).

He's absolutely right. Why do we attribute so much power to death when we believe it was conquered through Jesus's own death and resurrection? "Death has been trampled down by death," the church has proclaimed for centuries.

Paul proclaims, "When the perishable has been clothed with the imperishable, and the mortal with immortality, then the saying that is written will come true: "Death has been swallowed up in victory."[5]

God will conquer death; and yet, we seem convinced that it will also thwart his most daring plan and deepest desire. Jesus announces in Revelation, "I am the Living One; I was dead, and now look, I am alive for ever and ever! And I hold the keys of death and Hades."[6] Jesus holds the keys, and as Brad Jersak so acutely asks, "If Jesus now holds the keys of death and Hades, what do you think he'll do with them?"[7]

The resurrection brings hope to hopeless situations. It is hope that nothing is out of God's loving reach. As Jesus illustrates in the lost parables in Luke 15, God will keep seeking even if only one is lost. Perhaps this is partly why the early church hoped for God's mercy even after death; thus, "Since its inception, the church has prayed for the salvation of everyone, both in this life and on Judgment Day, including the dead!"[8] For the first several hundred years of the church this was a virtually universal practice.

The church dared this hope because, as Psalm 136 repeats over and over again, "His steadfast love endures forever."[9] Jeremiah echoes the sentiment, "The steadfast love of the Lord never ceases; his mercies never come to an end; they are new every morning; great is your faithfulness."[10]

If this is who God truly is, why should death have any say in the matter? If God is love, he is love regardless of whether we are dead or alive, in this life or the next. Christians believe that God "is the same yesterday and today and forever."[11] We don't believe that Jesus is the alpha, and death the omega; we believe Jesus gets the last word.

Yet, the God often portrayed in the evangelical gospel does a complete 180 after death. He is no longer merciful, his love ceases, and his patience wears thin. If this is the God we're dealing with, a God who says, "Love me

5. 1 Cor 15:54 (NIV).

6. Rev 1:18 (NIV).

7. Jersak, *Christlike God*, 247. Taken from *A More Christlike God*, by Brad Jersak. Copyright ©2015 by Plain Truth Ministries/CWRpress. Used by permission of Plain Truth Ministries, www.ptm.org

8. Jersak, *Her Gates*, 117.

9. Ps 136:1 (NRSV).

10. Lam 3:22-23 (NRSV).

11. Heb 13:8 (NRSV).

or I will torture you," then he sounds more like an abusive husband than a caring and loving one. (I don't think this is the image Jesus wanted us to have when he spoke of himself as the bridegroom of the Church). Imagine a woman who chose to stay in such a relationship. There would be fear and coercion, but could she ever trust that kind of a husband? Can we truly trust that kind of a God?

I can't. I tried, and it didn't work. I kept waiting for the other shoe to drop. In contrast, the beauty of the Gospel is that a God who remains the same through all eternity loves us. He loves us so much that he united himself with us in Christ. All of that falls apart if we insist that someday God's character will change. Then, the question becomes, which God is the real one?

This dilemma had me walking on eggshells for much of my life. I became very neurotic about my faith, fearing that if I didn't get the details right the "bad cop" would show up and make me miserable. I remember that I even avoided asking God for things in prayer for fear that he would deny them just to spite me. It might sound ridiculous to some, but if the God we teach resembles Jekyll and Hyde more than Jesus, it's difficult to relax around him.

Paul did not seem to share this difficulty, though he had much he was ashamed of. He referred to himself as the worst of sinners. After all, he used his religious fervor to harm those who were different from him. Then, one day, he had an encounter with God—not a violent or vengeful God—but a forgiving, victimized God who had but one question, "Why do you persecute me?"[12] God is forgiving. His love is set toward all people, no matter what they have done. "If we are faithless, he remains faithful—for he cannot deny himself."[13]

Paul experienced this extravagant love first hand, and this is why he could write with such conviction in Romans 8 that "in all these things we are more than conquerors through him who loved us. For I am convinced that neither death, nor life, nor angels, nor rulers, nor things present, nor things to come, nor powers, nor height, nor depth, nor anything else in all creation, will be able to separate us from the love of God in Christ Jesus our Lord."[14]

Did you catch that? Not even death can separate us from the love of Christ! And why should it; it has been trampled down by Jesus himself. Of course, many will say something like, "Paul is only talking about Christians

12. Acts 9:4 (NRSV).

13. 2 Tim 2:13 (NRSV).

14. Rom 8:37-39 (NRSV).

here. We can only stand on this foundation if we believe in him and have given our lives to him."

We have already seen what happens when we make God's salvation project depend on our faith response. It waters down the Gospel. But who is Paul talking about here? Here comes that word again: all. Paul tells us in chapter 3 that all have fallen short and are justified freely. He tells us in chapter 5 that "just as one trespass (by Adam) resulted in condemnation for all people, so also one righteous act (by Jesus) resulted in justification and life for all people."[15] So when Paul says nothing can separate us from God's love, he's talking about all of us. Otherwise, if any of us can be separated from his love, then we are (as the saying goes) "up a creek without a paddle."

The Father refuses to give up on his children, and he invites us to be as merciful and loving as he is. When we aren't merciful and loving, we begin to create chaos for ourselves. That chaos often becomes systemic and brings disaster to families, communities, and entire nations. This is why Jesus gives such dire warnings, but God never gives up.

The parable of the prodigal son is a perfect example of this, and is one of the most beautiful stories I have ever heard. I know I share this opinion with many others. I have definitely experienced life as both sons at points in my life. Because it is so beautiful, here it is from The Message in its entirety for anyone who is less familiar with it.

> "Then Jesus said, "There was once a man who had two sons. The younger said to his father, 'Father, I want right now what's coming to me.'
>
> "So the father divided the property between them. It wasn't long before the younger son packed his bags and left for a distant country. There, undisciplined and dissipated, he wasted everything he had. After he had gone through all his money, there was a bad famine all through that country and he began to hurt. He signed on with a citizen there who assigned him to his fields to slop the pigs. He was so hungry he would have eaten the corn cobs in the pig slop, but no one would give him any.
>
> "That brought him to his senses. He said, 'All those farmhands working for my father sit down to three meals a day, and here I am starving to death. I'm going back to my father. I'll say to him, Father, I've sinned against God, I've sinned before you; I don't deserve to be called your son. Take me on as a hired hand.' He got right up and went home to his father.
>
> "When he was still a long way off, his father saw him. His heart pounding, he ran out, embraced him, and kissed him.

15. Rom 5:18 (NIV).

The son started his speech: 'Father, I've sinned against God, I've sinned before you; I don't deserve to be called your son ever again.'

"But the father wasn't listening. He was calling to the servants, 'Quick. Bring a clean set of clothes and dress him. Put the family ring on his finger and sandals on his feet. Then get a grain-fed heifer and roast it. We're going to feast! We're going to have a wonderful time! My son is here—given up for dead and now alive! Given up for lost and now found!' And they began to have a wonderful time.

"All this time his older son was out in the field. When the day's work was done he came in. As he approached the house, he heard the music and dancing. Calling over one of the house-boys, he asked what was going on. He told him, 'Your brother came home. Your father has ordered a feast—barbecued beef!—because he has him home safe and sound.'

"The older brother stalked off in an angry sulk and refused to join in. His father came out and tried to talk to him, but he wouldn't listen. The son said, 'Look how many years I've stayed here serving you, never giving you one moment of grief, but have you ever thrown a party for me and my friends? Then this son of yours who has thrown away your money on whores shows up and you go all out with a feast!'

"His father said, 'Son, you don't understand. You're with me all the time, and everything that is mine is yours—but this is a wonderful time, and we had to celebrate. This brother of yours was dead, and he's alive! He was lost, and he's found!'"[16]

The story is quite astonishing. A son demands his share of the inheritance from his father. The inheritance was typically not divided up until the father had passed. Thus in a very real way the son was telling his father, "I wish you were dead." Or to put it another way, "Your existence has no impact on me."

I have sent this message to God myself. I have disregarded the truth of who I am in his eyes. The younger son in this story squandered his inheritance and ended up seeking table scraps. I didn't do any better. I was wasting away, starving for divine affection and affirmation. I didn't know it actually existed.

Yet the father had enduring patience for his son. When we get to know people, get to know their past and what they've endured, we begin to understand that they generally do what they think they need to in order to survive, even if the insanity is apparent to everyone around them. The father knew that his son genuinely didn't know any better. Jesus displayed

16. Luke 15:11-32 (MSG).

this same love and understanding when he cried out on the cross, "Father, forgive them; for they do not know what they are doing."[17]

Even after all the suffering, the hunger, and the humiliation, the son still didn't seem to get it. He decides to go back, but only because he needs a decent meal. He prepares a speech of contrition that seems to have a hint of manipulation mixed in. It's comforting to know I'm not the only thick-headed one.

Yet the father seems content to meet his son halfway. He's more than content, really. Read the father's reaction again. "When he was still a long way off, his father saw him. His heart pounding, he ran out, embraced him, and kissed him."

I know what it is to lose someone I love and care about, perhaps you do as well. Scenarios dart through your mind. Perhaps they'll realize what they've done and come back. Maybe one day they'll show up on the front porch, ready to restore a relationship. When it's someone you have poured your heart out for, especially a child, you never really give up. That's why this father saw his son while "he was still a long way off." He was waiting patiently. I imagine there were countless times when he thought he saw this son out of the corner of his eye, only to be disappointed. Then one day, his double take proved joyous. His son was home. Maybe he was still a selfish little brat who had much to learn. Either way, he had returned home to face his father, and that was a start.

I also know what it's like to mess up. We want things to go back to the way they were, but we know it's not that easy. We cringe anytime we are reminded of what we've done. We get defensive, not because we think our actions were justified, but because we fear that we've finally reached the last straw.

And then the son sees his father barreling toward him. His face is red, presumably with anger. The son prepares his speech in hopes that it will assuage his father's wrath. Before he can even begin, what he thought would be closed fists are revealed to be open hands embracing him. Against all reason, his father has never given up on him.

God understands our slow learning process and refuses ever to give up on us. This seems to be the case even at the end of the Bible in the book of Revelation.

At the end of Revelation, we see what we might expect to happen to sinners: "But as for the cowardly, the faithless, the polluted, the murderers, the fornicators, the sorcerers, the idolaters, and all liars, their place will be in the lake that burns with fire and sulfur, which is the second death."[18] We

---

17. Luke 23:34 (NRSV).

18. Rev 21:8 (NRSV).

might find it comforting to know that those who have done us wrong will pay for what they've done. Although, if you're like me, that list is maybe not very comforting. I have not murdered anyone, but I've been cowardly, faithless, and have certainly told my share of lies. When we realize that we have questionable behaviors to answer for, we grow very concerned. We once again assume that any talk of wrath has to do with God inflicting retribution on us. This is our natural reaction to reading about a lake of fire.

There is, however, some reason to doubt that the lake of fire is meant to be a picture of eternal torment, and evidence that it was a reference to the Dead Sea. Some ancient sources speak of the Dead Sea as a place of fire and sulfur which is a reminder of the fate suffered by Sodom and Gomorrah. Later in scripture, wickedness is often warned to lead to a similar fate. Brad Jersak writes, "We can see this in the ancient sources that describe the Dead Sea and remember its story. They note the ongoing evidence of subterranean fire and smoke as a reminder of the reality of judgment. To some, it was not merely a picture of the final place of judgment; the Dead Sea actually is the fiery lake of burning sulfur or a perpetual warning that what happened to Sodom could happen to anyone, even beloved Jerusalem!"[19]

In the end, however, God expresses the desire to restore even Sodom in the book of Ezekiel. It seems that nothing will make God finally give up on his creation, which explains what is described in the last chapter of Revelation.

> "Blessed are those who wash their robes, so that they will have the right to the tree of life and may enter the city by the gates. Outside are the dogs and sorcerers and fornicators and murderers and idolaters, and everyone who loves and practices falsehood."
>
> "It is I, Jesus, who sent my angel to you with this testimony for the churches. I am the root and the descendant of David, the bright morning star."
>
> The Spirit and the bride say, "Come." And let everyone who hears say, "Come." And let everyone who is thirsty come. Let anyone who wishes take the water of life as a gift."[20]

The city spoken of here is the New Jerusalem; it is the city that comes from heaven, whereby God makes his home in the world. It is a picture of the new creation. That is, rather than destroying everything, God makes all things new. We are told that the gates of this city will never be shut, and

19. Jersak, *Her Gates*, 83.
20. Rev 22:14-17 (NRSV).

that "nothing impure will ever enter it, nor will anyone who does what is shameful or deceitful, but only those whose names are written in the Lamb's book of life."[21]

A curious turn of events takes place, however, in this passage from the final chapter of Revelation. The people who were previously thrown into the lake of fire are now outside the gates of the city. Or perhaps, "To be outside the city walls is to be in the lake of fire."[22] The Spirit and the bride offer an invitation for them to enter the city and be healed; anyone who is thirsty can come in. Jersak surmises, "This vision declares the possibility and the hope that even in the next age, there are those whose thirst will finally bring them to say yes to the Lamb, even those who were unable to do so on this side of the grave."[23]

Once again, God refuses to give up. This shouldn't surprise us. As Paul reminds us, "Love never gives up, never loses faith, is always hopeful, and endures through every circumstance . . . love will last forever."[24] God is not a quitter.

I don't claim to know what exactly is going to happen when all is said and done. I don't know if everyone will end up experiencing eternal life, but I'm positive that God longs for that to be the case. I don't know exactly what's going to happen, but I believe that God will still be love, and that his mercy will never end. If we can't believe that, then we are on some very shaky ground. Whatever happens after death, it will not be dictated by death. I believe this because, as John Chrysostom expressed,

> "Let no one fear death, for the death of our Savior has set us free.
> He has destroyed it by enduring it. He destroyed hell when He
> descended into it. He put it into an uproar even as it tasted of
> His flesh."[25]

As Christians have sung for centuries in celebration of Jesus's resurrection,

> "Christ is risen from the dead,
> Trampling down death by death,
> And upon those in the tombs
> Bestowing life!"[26]

---

21. Rev 21:27 (NIV).

22. McDonald, *Evangelical Universalist*, 114.

23. Jersak, *Her Gates*, 172.

24. 1 Cor 13:7-8 (NLT).

25. Chrysostom, "The Easter Sermon of John Chrysostom," lines 38-42.

26. "Selected Liturgical Hymns," lines 1-2.

CHAPTER 17

Diluted Freedom

MY WIFE AND I love playing games together. We have a collection of board games we've been working on since we were dating in college. We really enjoy trivia games about movies or a television series. One of the challenges common in many trivia games is to identify a person based on a blurred picture. The image will initially be so fuzzy that nothing recognizable is present. Gradually the picture becomes clearer. If you wait until it's completely clear to give your answer, however, the time will be up, and you will lose.

My wife is amazing at this game. Most of the time, when she has given her correct answer all I can see is something resembling an abstract painting. I think I am currently losing to her something like two to seventy-nine, give or take a few.

This game is similar to the way we often understand the Gospel and present it to others. People are given a chance to decide that Jesus is the Son of God. The problem is that his image is often blurred by pain, suffering, and misrepresentation. Many people wonder how there can possibly be a good God when there is so much evil in the world, or when people they love have been allowed to hurt for so long.

As we looked in last chapter, someday many Christians believe that the timer will go off. Unless a person has given an answer before the image becomes perfectly clear, the game will be lost. Some Christians explain this scenario by affirming free will. They affirm that somehow each of us has the ability to make the right decision, and that makes us responsible.

Some Christians disagree, however, on whether or not people can decide for Christ after death. Many Christians hold to an "age of accountability" that was mentioned in the previous chapter. Others argue that anyone who was not presented with the Gospel will not be held accountable for their lack of opportunity. Those who disagree assert that any who have not given their lives to Christ will be held accountable, regardless of whether or not they have heard about him. They will say there is no biblical precedent for giving them a pass in scripture. To be fair, however, there is no scriptural warrant for giving children under the age of twelve a pass either. As it turns out, we can be pretty arbitrary with our beliefs at times.

All of this impacts our idea of free will. But how free are we, really? Is a woman who grew up in a predominantly Muslim country immersed in Muslim ideals and culture really as free as me—a boy raised in the Church in a country that claims to be Christian—to choose Jesus? That doesn't seem to be very compassionate. In that instance, it feels as though I was allowed to start the race a few miles ahead.

Of course, this notion of free will doesn't just apply to our faith decision for Christ. It also applies to our ability to make right decisions and to correct our behavior. Growing up in the church, I know full well that it is filled with people stuck in destructive patterns and hurtful behaviors. Some of these behaviors are talked about and addressed often; others can hide below the surface and even masquerade as healthy and appropriate. Either way, the message is the same: you have free will to do what's right, so if you'd simply try harder and believe more faithfully, you could behave differently. When this doesn't happen, people are filled with shame at their failures.

Is this really accurate though? How free are we? Let's take a hypothetical example of a tragic, but all too common, scenario. What if a young girl was sexually abused by her father? The very man who was supposed to take care of her violates her trust and innocence. Let's say that because of the trauma she has experienced, she cannot bring herself to believe that there is a God who would allow the suffering she endured, especially not a God identified as Father. Her trauma also makes it virtually impossible for her to be vulnerable or intimate with anyone. She hides it well, but deep down she is incredibly lonely and depressed. At some point she tumbles into alcoholism to numb the pain.

Is she free to give up the alcohol? What about other victims of sexual abuse that find relief in sexual promiscuity with many different partners? Are they free to give up their behavior? We are so influenced by our past experiences, the people around us, and the culture in which we live. When we speak of having free will, we connect it with the notion that we can be autonomous beings, free from being impacted by people and situations, environments and experiences. In reality, such unaffected people don't exist.

One of the problems with our typical notion of free will is that it turns faith into an exam, and a remarkably unfair exam at that. In college, some professors were definitely better than others. At times we could listen to the lectures, read all the textbooks, and still confront material on the exam that was never covered. Imagine trying to do this with blurry glasses that prevented us from seeing clearly, or ear plugs that made the lectures unintelligible? This is why the way we often describe the Gospel falls short of its true beauty. If we are held accountable for our ability to identify a blurry image, all while being confined by influences beyond our control, we're describing a God who enjoys failing his students rather than helping them succeed.

Thankfully, this is not the Abba that Jesus portrays. This is not what Jesus is preparing us for. The offer Jesus is making is more holistic and transformational. That's what we need. For example, take this offer that Jesus extends:

> "Are you tired? Worn out? Burned out on religion? Come to me. Get away with me and you'll recover your life. I'll show you how to take a real rest. Walk with me and work with me—watch how I do it. Learn the unforced rhythms of grace. I won't lay anything heavy or ill-fitting on you. Keep company with me and you'll learn to live freely and lightly."[1]

As someone who is deeply impacted by anxiety, it doesn't help to ask me an exam question like, "Where will you go if you die tonight?" It initiates my fight or flight instinct and leads me to insecurity and shame. It makes the problem worse. But the idea that I can live freely and lightly is like hot chocolate on a winter day. What's ironic is that when I thought some of my requirements to pass the test were to talk to other people about God, I couldn't bring myself to do it. I was miserable, and I didn't want to make others share in the pain. On the other hand, when I realized that God was offering something deeper, I couldn't stop talking about him. I could finally see how good he was.

HEALING FROM TRAUMA

Freedom is an amazing thing. Tragically, the way the church often speaks of freedom is more shaming than it is emancipating. God offers freedom, not freedom to pass a test, but freedom from the debilitating scars we've endured, the lies we've lived in, and the dysfunctions that arise from them. It is not a quick fix; it is a healing process. This is what we need, but much of the church world has been oblivious to it.

---

1. Matt 11:28-30 (MSG).

Much of our need for healing stems from trauma we have endured. There is no one qualification for trauma. That misunderstanding was part of my obstacle. I figured that, because I had never endured more obvious instances of trauma, like physical abuse, that I had nothing in my life to debilitate me. But as Teresa B. Pasquale assures us, "Your hurt is valid and as deeply traumatic as you feel it is. Your experience is valid, and your hurt is real."[2]

Trauma can come in many forms. It can be physical, emotional, or spiritual. It can take place on a battlefield, within a community, or in the privacy of your own home. It can involve family members, trusted leaders, or complete strangers. Post-Traumatic Stress is often associated with war veterans, but it is much more common than that. It can affect anyone. When it does, it locks people into their threat mode and can impact the way they behave and think at a deep level.

When we are threatened, we instinctively develop ways to protect ourselves. Many who have felt abandoned as children will develop defense mechanisms to ensure they are not hurt again. They may leave relationships or communities before things get too comfortable. In my case, I learned how to adapt to my surroundings and fulfill any expectations. Often these expectations were completely in my head, but I was planning for anything that could go wrong.

This is the way we survive. It stems from our fight or flight response. Some play out their survival mechanisms by freezing or submitting. Either way, we become hyper sensitive to actions around us and filter them through our survival mode. As Pasquale explains, someone fixed in this mode "sees danger everywhere."[3] This happened often in the early years of our marriage. I believed any moment of anger or sadness could threaten what we had, so I would assume my wife was angry with me even when she wasn't.

The point I am hoping to convey is that there are so many ways that our past and people in our lives influence us, for good or for ill. This impacts the way we behave in ways that we cannot see and often cannot control. So to speak of people as being responsible for all of this due to a judicial notion of free will is not helpful. Instead of empowering, it tends to bring more shame. There is, however, a helpful way to speak of freedom and responsibility, and we will look at that later.

This shame can be weighty and overwhelming. We already are prone to believing lies about ourselves. When we are convinced that all of our tendencies and choices are the result of cognitive, deliberate decisions, we

2. Pasquale, *Sacred Wounds*, 23.

3. Ibid, 25.

naturally think of ourselves as rotten people. We lose sight of our identities as dearly loved children. We have to know and remember who we are deep down, and that no number of failures or scars can change it.

We are so impacted by our environment, especially in our younger years. In his book *The Face of Social Suffering*, Merrill Singer writes about a street drug addict he calls Tony.[4] In Tony's instance, drugs were not chosen out of desire or curiosity. Instead he was introduced to them by his father. This helped lead into deeper drug habits, gang life, and extensive prison terms. Tony was deeply influenced, as we all are, by his surroundings and his family. To say Tony had "free will" to make all the choices he made is true in some sense, but it is also misleading. Based on his research, Singer writes, "It is neither a coincidence nor some strange social concentration of poor character or immorality that explains why people who lead lives like Tony's disproportionately come from poor and working class-backgrounds and are the victims of early child abuse."[5] Trauma has profound impact on our development and behavior.

Our behaviors are not only dictated by trauma. They can simply be the result of adapting to our environment in necessary, albeit sometimes unhealthy ways. We are often, as the colloquial phrase asserts, products of our environment, especially until we experience some self-awareness. It is incredibly helpful to see and understand these patterns. On the flip side, however, it is emotionally and spiritually crippling to condemn someone for these ways of handling life.

The enneagram has been immensely insightful for me in this area. There are nine types in the enneagram, and each type develops in response to a childhood wound. My type, the Four, typically had a sense of abandonment or being misunderstood as a child. Often this comes not from an overt act of abandonment but from what the child perceives as such. It is not about blaming, but understanding that we are human and are deeply impacted by those around us. Parents are dealing with their own issues, but children often can't help but assume it is about them.

As a result of my childhood wound, I came to believe that there was something innately wrong or flawed in me. This manifests at times as withdrawing inward to avoid rejection and closing myself off to those around me. It's not very healthy behavior, but it is the result of childhood adaptations that I never understood. There are times still when something will trigger my sense of being defective, and my emotions will take over. Just like

4. Reprinted by permission of Waveland Press, Inc. from Singer. THE FACE OF SOCIAL SUFFERING: THE LIFE HISTORY OF A STREET DRUG ADDICT. Long Grove, IL: Waveland Press, Inc., © 2006 All rights reserved.

5. Ibid, 146.

Jesus's accusers, I know not what I do. It takes time to snap out of it. Thankfully I have grown with the love of my wife, family, and the help of spiritual mentors. They do not shame me for these behaviors, because shame is the root cause.

RESTORED WILL

We believe that God has created us to have free will, but our current wills are perhaps not as free as we think. If a woman chooses to stay in an abusive relationship, we don't call that freedom, we call that self-destructive behavior. If a man continues time and again to gamble, knowing that it is costing him his life and family, we don't see that as a rational decision. We call it being controlled. Paul called this being a "slave to sin."[6] The idea of free will must be better than that.

Let's put it another way. Genesis tells us that God created us in his image. When he created us, he saw that we were good. Our typical notion of free will is that it offers us a fifty-fifty chance at choosing what is right and healthy. Imagine someone is presented with the opportunity to begin using meth. Would we idealize a free will that took time to analyze the situation? No, of course not, because a healthy person would not take any time making the decision. She would immediately refuse, not wanting to bring pain and destruction on her and her loved ones. For someone to be created good, and in God's image, she would need to have a will that desired good, right, and healthy things.

Thus when someone chooses to act in self-sabotaging ways, this is not an expression of a free will, but a distorted one. Adam and Eve don't eat the apple out of freedom, they eat it out of fear, and out of a blindness to who they are in God. The reverse is also true; we find healing in seeing who we truly are. Take Paul's experience for example. Paul did not stop persecuting the church out of guilt or regret, but because he had a moment where he saw things as they were. He then was stricken with blindness, representing his true problem. He later is said to tell Timothy that "I received mercy because I had acted ignorantly in unbelief."[7] His fundamental problem was that he did not know or see things as they truly were.

Brad Jersak writes that for many church fathers, better than "will" was a higher faculty called "*nous*" in Greek, or an orientation toward love. Jersak explains, God "has planted within every one of his children a capacity for love that is perfectly designed to respond to God's love when we encounter

6. Rom 7:14 (NIV).

7. 1 Tim 1:13 (NRSV).

it. This is the default mode of the true humanity: not a neutral freedom of will to respond to or reject God, but a responsive propensity—a willingness of heart—to love the Lover when we see that Love for who and what he is."[8]

What we see, then, is that our wills are not as free as we would like to think, but need to be restored to and reunited with the state that seeks love and grace as God designed us to. Can we have that in this life amidst all the pain and confusion? I believe we can have those moments, by God's grace. That's the healing he desires. It is all by grace, so if we can believe that God's mercy is big enough for children who cannot make informed decisions, surely his mercy would extend to those whose faculties have been distorted by trauma as well.

Pouring guilt and shame on someone for behaviors done out of pain or blindness is not helpful. It is yet another contributing factor to our patterns of avoidance. We need to face ourselves, and this becomes much harder to do when we believe God simply wants to blame and accuse. I kept many dark secrets hidden for that very reason, and they ate me up inside.

We do need freedom, but it comes through a difficult journey, and only a merciful and loving God can lead us there. Thankfully, as Kallistos Ware reassures, "The power that is victorious is the power of loving compassion, and so it is a victory that does not overrule but enhances our human freedom."[9]

8. Jersak, "Free Will," para. 16.
9. Ware, "Dare We Hope," para. 28.

PART V

RACING TOWARD THE STARTING LINE

CHAPTER 18

The Pain We Always Avoid

I WALKED SEVERAL LAPS of the circular mall in the next town from our home, not sure what to make of what was happening to my life. My wife had put her foot down on my dysfunctional behaviors, refusing to wear the ring I had placed on her hand again until something changed. That wouldn't have been so bad if I actually knew what those behaviors were. Unfortunately, I was still completely blind to them. My head hung down in defeat, gazing across the worst conglomeration of carpet patterns one could imagine. The various carpet sections patched together were chaotic at best. If nothing else, it mirrored the chaos of my fragile world. Somehow, I would have to confront my darkness.

Much of that darkness began as a child. I learned then that it was difficult to get along in the church world when you were asking too many questions or acting out of line. As a pastor's kid I also learned that our financial well-being was partly dependent on my ability to be a dutiful follower. So I learned to be what people wanted me to be. From child, to teenager, to college student, I became adept at shutting my heart down in order to please those around me. The sad thing was I thought this ability was a strength or virtue. What I came to learn was that, while these behaviors helped me survive in some difficult situations, they were not conducive to a healthy marriage.

We all have our ways of dealing with life and conflicts. We get accustomed to them, and cannot imagine living any other way. In fact, we dread living any other way. As Richard Rhor asserts, "We really are our own worst enemies, and salvation is primarily from ourselves. It seems humans would sooner die than change or admit that they are mistaken."[1]

1. Rhor, *Breathing Under Water*, xix.

That's the difficult part to accept: we are our worst enemies. It would be so much simpler if we could just blame everyone else. The problem is that, though the insults and lies may originate with someone else, soon we become the cheer captain. The lies follow us as our inner voice absorbs them. We are often blind to their source, however, and project them onto people around us.

As we talked about in the last chapter, we all develop ways of getting through life with subtle and subconscious techniques. It's not our fault, it's just what happens. In many cases it wasn't anyone's fault. The ones who hurt us were often simply living from their own false narratives. The reality is that if we want to move on from those patterns and behaviors, it has to be our decision to do so. It's not our fault that we've arrived here, but it usually is our patterns that keep us stuck. Our dysfunctions feel normal, even comfortable, and this desire to stay where we are is going to hurt us.

This is why, for the most part, people don't change until they have to, until they hit the proverbial rock bottom. Richard Rhor elaborates, "Until you bottom out, and come to the limits of your own fuel supply, there is no reason for you to switch to a higher octane of fuel. For that is what is happening! Why would you? You will not learn to actively draw upon a Larger Source until your usual resources are depleted and revealed as wanting. In fact, you will not even know there is a Larger Source until your own sources and resources fail you."[2]

We usually are not willing to rethink our patterns until they've caused us enough pain. For a long time my defense mechanisms served me quite well. I was successful in college, and people thought well of me. I played the game effectively. It wasn't until I was faced with how much pain I was actually causing myself and those around me that I would even consider a different strategy. Only when I was faced with this suffering and inability to be happy was I willing to lean on grace.

This seems to be a lesson that Paul had to learn as well. Paul, formerly known as Saul, was pretty sure of himself at one time. By his own account he kept the Jewish law blamelessly and had quite the reputation. Only after facing an intense difficulty, what he called the "thorn in my flesh," was he able to discover this truth: "I will boast all the more gladly of my weaknesses, so that the power of Christ may dwell in me . . . for whenever I am weak, then I am strong."[3]

The church often misses this message. We still get caught in the trap of correlating difficulties with God's disapproval. We have an even harder

2. Ibid, 3.

3. 2 Cor 12:9-10 (NRSV).

time finding God's redemptive love at work in our moral failures. But without those, we would remain blind to our self-sabotaging ways. As Julian of Norwich so refreshingly put it, "First we fall and later we see it: and both of the Mercy of God."[4]

We don't want to see the patterns that make us fall. Thus we are dealing with a lack of sight, and until we stub our toe, we think we're doing just fine. It's curious that on the cross Jesus didn't pray, "Father forgive them, even though they're wicked." Instead he says that it's their ignorance that leads them to act in such selfish and hurtful ways. If they could only see, they would drop what they were doing and repent.

That's why we need to allow people to hit rock bottom. The problem is the church doesn't give room for this. We are so obsessed with having right behavior. But why wouldn't we be? We think God's acceptance of us depends on it. I've sat and listened to sermons and talks about the unconditional love, unlimited patience, and unending mercy of God. But what would some of those preachers say if we asked them, "What'll happen to someone who doesn't accept God's love and dies tomorrow?" All of a sudden, God's love has conditions, he's lost his patience, and his mercy has left the building.

When we are convinced that God's love is so fickle, we become uncomfortable with anything that could jeopardize our chances. We begin condemning anything inside ourselves that is ugly and selfish. We push it aside. We might encounter people who can keep us accountable, but often a shallow notion of accountability simply results in suppressing what's really going on inside. We often do this as faith communities as well. We bury the unpleasant realities by pushing people aside, or by pretending everything's okay when we get together. All of this tends to make the problem worse.

Jesus addressed this, as he so often did, with a parable:

"When the unclean spirit has gone out of a person, it wanders through waterless regions looking for a resting place, but it finds none. Then it says, 'I will return to my house from which I came.' When it comes, it finds it empty, swept, and put in order. Then it goes and brings along seven other spirits more evil than itself, and they enter and live there; and the last state of that person is worse than the first. So will it be also with this evil generation."[5]

When we just push issues aside because they make us uncomfortable, we neglect to solve the problem, or to fill ourselves with anything of substance. The problem just returns, albeit often manifested in other ways. We end up becoming blind to why we are so grumpy, irritable, or anxious. This

---

4. Norwich, *Revelations*, 3481.

5. Matt 12:43-45 (NRSV).

is why Richard Rhor would say, "I do not think you should get rid of your sin until you have learned what it has to teach you."[6] Our patterns and dysfunctions can enlighten us on what's really going on inside. If that were not the case, I would still be oblivious to my own inner world.

But again, the church often doesn't make room for this. To change that, we need to see the truth of how God feels about us and our problems. We've taught that God is uncomfortable or unable to be amongst our sin. The reality is that he's much more willing and able to bear with our less attractive parts than we are. We bury. We condemn. We push aside. I have a closet full of skeletons and assumed that they were fueling God's anger toward me. In reality, he's much more comfortable with them than I am. He embraces them. He loves them. He speaks tenderly to them. He dines with them. The only way through to the other side is to pull up a seat and participate in what God is doing in my closet.

The first time I met with my spiritual director he nearly had me falling off my chair. He was speaking about the importance of bearing our sin, looking at it, and learning from it. He said that our tendency is to try and fix whatever we see is malfunctioning inside of us. When we do this, however, we miss out on what it has to teach us. Then he dropped the bomb, "Our sin can save us."

That just about fried my circuit board. I had been taught that any sin and infirmities within us were to be avoided, condemned, and set aside. I learned that God wanted a holy life from us, which typically meant going to church and avoiding anything "worldly."

When Jesus went to the cross, he was bearing our sin, our shame, our anxiety, and our illusions. He bore them, not to prevent us from having to bear them, but to show us how to bear them properly. Our sin, our weaknesses, and selfishness is what reveals to us the core problem: we don't know that we are intimately and fundamentally loved by God, cherished by God, and united to God through the incarnation. We are blind to this reality. That blindness manifests itself in all our less attractive behaviors. If we could only see the truth, we would change.

We cannot see it because all the garbage whirling around within convinces us that we are people God simply couldn't love. This is why Jesus emphasizes repentance. Repentance is about seeing differently, having a different mind, so we can see who God really is and what he thinks about us. We do this by having the courage to look at our unsightly scars and behaviors and by trusting that Jesus is already there. We must be willing to face our pain.

6. Rhor, *Falling Upward*, 61.

Let's go back to Plato's cave for a moment. If you recall, the prisoners in the cave could only see the shadows of what was passing back and forth in front of the fire. That was their entire reality. They didn't know any of those entities for what they were. They attributed names and titles to these images out of their own perceptions.

Rabbi Shemuel ben Nachmani wrote in the Talmud, "A man is shown in a dream only what is suggested by his own thoughts."[7] That is, our perception dictates how we see things. In the cave analogy, the shadows on the wall were not seen objectively. Instead, they were experienced through the filter of each prisoner's presuppositions. It's not much different for us. We like to think that we are rational beings who perceive the world around us impartially and accurately. That's not usually the case.

This lack of self-understanding was a significant factor during the difficult time of my marriage. Our communication was completely inept. It wasn't that we weren't talking to each other; it was that no matter how much we talked, we could not truly hear each other. We both entered into our marriage with scars and bruises from our past. The noise from these internal struggles drowned out what we were saying to each other.

In any relational conflict, our instinct is to think that the other person is the issue. We tell ourselves that they just aren't listening or trying hard enough to convey their thoughts. The reality, however, is that the relationship contains only what we bring into it. The baggage is within each one of us.

Our tendency is to run away from that possibility. We will only get where we want to go, however, if we choose to face it. Again, imagine the prisoner from the cave after he has been set free. He exits the confines of what he has known to be confronted with what's true. Everything he has ever believed was a lie, and it was all from his perception.

That is the truth we all must be willing to face to move forward. If we don't, the things we are blind to will end up controlling and twisting us into someone we were never meant to be. Through our marriage difficulties, the ensuing counseling, and all the expeditions into healing and self-discovery that so many have traveled with me, I uncovered some jarring truths. For one, most of my life challenges were a direct result of my defense mechanisms, which were themselves direct results of my shame and insecurities. That's unsettling at first, or probably for a while. But eventually my eyes were opened to the truth that my deepest negative perceptions of myself and of how God looked at me were all a facade, and I didn't have to be controlled by them anymore. It's an incredible journey that we are all invited into, but

7. "Babylonian Talmud: Tractate Berakoth," lines 74-5.

we must also take the route through the dark alleys of the pain and shadow within us. That is the only way.

There are patterns within the church that undermine this process, however, and leave us stunted in our development. One of those patterns is what a professor and mentor of mine used to call "offering God a promissory note" when we mess up. We tell God how sorry we are and that we promise to do better in the future. This is the focus of many church services I have experienced. We think the heart of the Gospel is acting Christian, so we quickly push any mistakes aside so we can try again tomorrow. But maybe it is our striving that is the problem.

Another popular feature of church services that I've experienced is casting away our sins because of what Jesus has gone through on the cross. Sometimes this takes the form of writing down our sins and nailing them to a cross to be done with them. Other times the papers are thrown into a fire to be burned. It is absolutely true that the cross saves us from condemnation, but as we looked at before, the condemnation is ours, not God's. He is always for us, always seeking to redeem us. The cross offers freedom from sin, but that freedom has to come through dying to our egos and selfishness. We must face our darkness and allow the humiliation of that to completely disarm our egos. That is the necessary death. We must go through death to get to resurrection. So these practices can be helpful as long as they don't lead us to skip past the necessary step of facing our darkness.

Most of the time we end up hiding our sin and pretending it doesn't exist. As a mentor once explained, it is like holding a beach ball under the water. You can do it, but it's going to take pretty much all your energy to succeed, leaving you with little energy for anything else. Unfortunately, in my experience, the church often encourages people to do this very thing. We hide our pain, our depression, and our screw ups because we fear what God will do. When God was the monster in my closet, I could bring myself to do nothing else. As Rhor explains, "You will never turn your will and your life over to any other kind of God except a loving and merciful one. Why would you? But now that you know, why would you not . . . it is easy to surrender when you know that nothing but Love and Mercy are on the other side."[8]

Our first step is to simply be honest about the murky waters in our souls. We need to open up about the things that fill us with fear and with shame. This very weekend I was drowning in my anxiety. There was anger and bitterness filling up in me because of a conflict I had during the week. I couldn't figure out why I was incapable of letting it go. I would push it down only for it to creep up again. Over and over I would catch myself having

---

8. Rhor, *Breathing Under Water*, 27.

hypothetical arguments in my head trying to defend myself. It wasn't until I quieted down and sat still in prayer that I realized I was deeply ashamed for experiencing these emotions. I was trying to hide them for fear of suffering chastisement from God. But only by owning up to them was I able to experience the truth: God's mercy triumphs, always.

We spend so much effort hiding our darkness from God, much like Adam and Eve did. We don't really believe that God's love will overcome it. It is only when we look at our crap, our baggage, whatever we call it within the understanding of God's infinite love that we will realize how loved we really are. When we bury it, we presume we are loved because we can make things look presentable. Oh, but how refreshing it is to enter in the closet, see our darkness for what it is, and yet find that God's love remains secure.

We must ultimately get fed up with faking and hiding to do this. We must hit rock bottom, and the church must make room for this if it wants people truly to bring themselves to the table. This healing process takes time and patience. It involves failures and setbacks. All that really means is that the religious facade we were so proud of wasn't working, and we can finally get rid of it. Maybe, instead of acting like it is the end of the world when someone reverts or backslides, we can rejoice that they are finally on the path to recovery. Maybe my failures mean that I am ready to stop being so miserable and admit that I really do want the grace God is holding out to me.

We have such a beautiful picture of God's patience in the story of the prodigal son, and just as much with the older brother. This latter brother thought he had it all together. He thought he had the system all figured out. He would just slave away and certainly earn his father's affection. It's obvious that he had been harboring bitterness and rage for years. Finally, when his younger brother returns from his scandalous escapades only to be celebrated, the older brother reaches his limit. He hits his rock bottom. He realizes all his efforts have been in vain, and he explodes on his father. "Look! All these years I've been slaving for you and never disobeyed your orders. Yet you never gave me even a young goat so I could celebrate with my friends. But when this son of yours who has squandered your property with prostitutes comes home, you kill the fattened calf for him!"[9]

How are we to classify this outburst from the older son? Was it disrespectful? Was he backsliding from his dutiful behavior? If we view God as a vindictive taskmaster, we would have to say yes. But if God is patient, and understands the ebb and flow to our spiritual growth, perhaps he does not see it that way. Maybe he condones it. Maybe he actually celebrates it as a

9. Luke 15:29-30 (NIV).

step towards wholeness. Perhaps in his heart he is saying, "Finally, my son shared what's in his heart with me. Finally, he stopped pretending. Now we can move forward. Now, he can see how deep my love is."

The purpose of our faith is not to become the most religious people we can be, but to realize how loved we are right here, right now, even in the midst of our darkness. In fact, we need our darkness and hang-ups because they are what wakes us up to the facade we're living in. When we learn to sit with our skeletons, and realize that God has been with them all along, our facade begins to fade. We experience how loved we really are. That is the sacred space where freedom grows.

CHAPTER 19

Encountering Presence

THE EVANGELICAL CHURCH, FOR better or worse, has been my religious stomping ground all of my life. It has been the source of some of my greatest encounters and, simultaneously, my most painful moments. It's a complicated relationship. Yet I am still here. My personality is one that likes to be connected to the past. I don't want to be handcuffed by it, but neither do I want to be severed from it and forget where I come from, or all that I've been through.

One of the weaknesses of the evangelical church is that it hasn't commonly sought or even desired a connection with its past (though this is changing). My tribe has a heritage linked to the holiness movement of the 1800s and refers back to the leaders of that movement. We usually look back as far as John Wesley of the 1700s. This is better than nothing, but considering that the Christian-Judeo tradition goes back several thousand years, we end up severed from our roots.

God is not merely relegated to our faith tradition, though. We believe in a God who is everywhere, all the time. We believe that he reveals himself through his creation and has been doing so since the beginning of time. He has been speaking to his children through all the ages, and he continues to do so. That is why, especially at a mystical level, there is so much truth that is shared and agreed upon across many world religions.

If we could at least settle on the belief that God is always present around us, that would be a start. The problem is, as much as we confess this to be true, we don't actually live by it. In practice, Christians often portray God as being contained in their churches or in their Bibles. Thus, our spiritual practices can sometimes be limiting, or at least they were for me. Fortunately, if we are willing to look back, we have a large tradition of practices that can help us live out our belief that God is within and around us always.

CONFESSION

One practice that has been common throughout church history is confession. It is, however, sorely lacking in the evangelical church. This is partly because historically we have thought being descendants of the reformation somehow makes us better than our predecessors. There are still, sadly, many Protestants who refuse to acknowledge Catholics as brothers and sisters in Christ. We therefore stigmatize many of the Catholic practices merely because they are, well, Catholic.

Evangelicals are also down on confession because of our private approach to our spirituality. It's just "God and me" in our usual approach to faith. While it is true that we must know God's love for us so deeply that we do not require admiration and validation by another person, it is also paradoxically true that we cannot get to this point without the help of others. A true spiritual friend on the journey is someone who will tell us what we need to hear, with no demand that we adhere to her words.

The practice of confession involves verbalizing one's sins to a priest and hearing that they are absolved. For some Christians, it involves doing the same with a spiritual mentor or trusted friend. Many Evangelicals, however, will give the argument that "I only need to confess my sins to God." We see confessing as shackling ourselves to the validation of others. We conclude that the solution is asserting our freedom in God's forgiveness.

We do know that we can't live up to our potential without others; however, so we attempt to help the process through what are commonly known as accountability groups. There is a confessional element to these groups, and they often bring immense benefits. The problem that sometimes arises is a performance-based mentality whereby we rely on our own efforts to improve our behavior. This can often lead to shame and embarrassment when this is the primary focus, which is why many people end up withholding and concealing their baggage.

For all our talk about grace and acceptance, we are often obsessed with our spiritual performance and Christian behavior. The problem, as we've looked at throughout this book, is that we tend to believe in a conditional salvation rather than a participatory one. When I've asked God for forgiveness in the past, I've quickly followed it with a promise to do better. I've done so with a "don't hurt me, I'll never do it again" attitude, fearful of the consequences of my screwing up. Such dread never brings out the best in us.

That's why a good confession is founded on unconditional love. Before we can hope to change, we have to truly know that our place in God's heart doesn't depend on it. Otherwise the burden is too overwhelming and weighs us down.

The first time I shared my darkest thoughts with my spiritual director was one of the scariest things I've ever done. I had spent so many years hiding and pretending to the people around me. My sense of self-worth was completely warped because of it.

I had spoken to him about confession a few months earlier. Confession to another person, especially a priest, was highly stigmatized in my church heritage, so I wanted to feel it out first. He assured me that nothing I shared with him would make him care any less or think differently of me. Priests have heard many confessions in their time, so we're hard pressed to share anything that will truly shock them.

As our next meeting was approaching, I was preparing to share my deepest feelings, failures, and scars with him. I pulled into the parking lot knowing that I needed to move forward. Even still, I contemplated driving away and never returning. I was so nervous.

Once the floodgates were open, however, I couldn't stop talking. I was astonished that no matter what I shared with him, the compassion in his eyes never wavered. I cried like I had been storing up tears for ages. "That's my baggage," I concluded, unable to think of anything else to share.

In his prayer room are icons of different saints of the church. He began to speak to me about some of their backgrounds and shortcomings. "You're in good company," he assured me. "None of them are any better than you are. You belong."[1] I had never felt so thankful to be like everyone else before in my life.

I can't adequately describe how moving the experience was, but the pattern of confession isn't just in those monumental moments. I had to learn how to live in a confessional way with my wife. That doesn't mean that I make her carry all my scars and pains, but I'm learning to at least let her help. I wasn't very good at that for a long time. Anytime a trusted friend genuinely asks how we're doing, and we shove our pain aside by saying, "I'm fine," we are missing out on the confessional life. We are robbing ourselves of the relief of knowing we're not the only ones having a bad day, or who are depressed, or ashamed.

We're also robbing ourselves of the intimate knowledge that we are loved in our pain, not in spite of it. It leads us to the true goal of spirituality, which "is actually not the perfect avoidance of all sin, which is not possible

---

1. If you are familiar with the Enneagram, you know how much these words mean to a type four.

anyway (1 John 1:8–9; Romans 5:12), but the struggle itself, and the encounter and wisdom that comes from it."[2]

THE JESUS PRAYER

Another way that Christians for centuries have sought to encounter God is by repeating a prayer called the "Jesus prayer". The Jesus prayer is as follows:

"Lord Jesus Christ, Son of God, have mercy on me, a sinner."

This prayer can sound awkward at first. To some ears it can sound self-deprecating, as if it's begging God to forgive us for being terrible, rotten people, so I'll explain the understanding I've come to of this prayer, with help from many who have come before me.

"Lord Jesus Christ, Son of God": Confessing Jesus as Lord is consenting to his way of working in our lives. It is giving up our own efforts in order to rely on him. It is also confessing that, though he is our Lord, he shares in our humanity and sympathizes with our struggles in a personal and universal way. He is Son of God, so he unites our humanity to divinity. We are not left to remain where we are, but through letting go of our own way, we discover our true identity in God.

Then comes the more difficult portion of the prayer: "Have mercy on me, a sinner." Today when we hear the word mercy, we usually think of receiving pardon for an offense. This is part of what biblical mercy is, but not the main aspect. Mercy has to do with helping someone in a difficult or desperate circumstance. For example, the Good Samaritan was someone who showed great mercy to the man attacked by robbers.

Lastly, the term sinner does not fundamentally describe someone who violates ethical norms. Instead, as we looked at in chapter 4, sin is about living outside of our identity as loved and accepted by God. Therefore we could paraphrase the prayer like this: "Lord Jesus Christ, Son of God, you have become one with us. By uniting us with you, you have shown me who I really am. But I forget that I am included in your life, and that I am loved unconditionally. When I forget, my life becomes chaotic, and I don't live as I want to. Please help me to remember who I truly am in you and to live from that reality, and thank you for forgiving me when I don't."

It has been important for me to remember this meaning of the prayer as I repeat it. It is also helpful to be able to repeat the shorter, original version.

This serves as a kind of chant that allows us to turn off our usually unhelpful patterns of thinking. Maybe it's self-deprecating thoughts, judgmental thoughts, or comparing thoughts. Either way, they have not moved

2. Rhor, *Breathing Under Water*, 31.

us very far along. Chants have a way of bypassing them for a time. This is why they are a common practice across most religious traditions.

A further benefit of chants or repeated phrases is that it floods our psyche with beauty and grace. Our minds are flooded with plenty of thoughts anyway, most of them below the surface. Many of these are negative and debilitating. We might as well get some good stuff in there.

The repetition has a way of breaking down our walls. When we are down on ourselves, we become adept at dismissing compliments or restorative words said by others. This further drives us into despair.

One day I was sitting in my therapist's office discussing the challenges I was facing. I talked about having a tendency to assume that any negative situations are because of me.

I've learned that I have a tendency to do this because of childhood experiences and the way I interpreted them when I was young. Because of this, I have taken every relationship failure and negative experience as a confirmation that I was somehow inherently flawed.

I kept digging deeper and deeper, but finally my therapist stopped me and asked, "Are you a bad person?"

I was taken aback a bit, and frankly frustrated. I was on a roll. As an enneagram four, I can swim in melancholy for days and be perfectly content. I just wanted him to let me ramble, but I answered the question as honestly as I knew how.

"Well, I know the right answer is no. I know those around me would not say I'm a bad person. But it feels wrong to say that."

He pressed into my answer, "Why does that feel wrong?"

"Well, I have bad thoughts sometimes," I explained.

"Everyone struggles with that."

"I've made a lot of mistakes," I insisted.

"Everyone has."

I didn't know what to say. Again he asked me, "Are you a bad person? Are you a bad person? Are you a bad person?" As he kept posing the question, this sensation came over me—as though I had a gaping wound in my heart. I had ignored it for who knows how long, but now it was being exposed. I wept like a baby. I was completely vulnerable in front of this man who would not let me keep beating myself up.

Then he began repeating, "You're not a bad person. You're not a bad person. It's all a big lie. You're not a bad person." For the next several minutes he kept repeating this, over and over again. This was a life changing moment for me. I had lived much of my life believing there was something inherently wrong with me, and keeping people at a distance so they couldn't see it. That day my therapist's repeated message broke through my wall. It was a step for me to see that, as Kallistos Ware reminds us, "in their inner essence all created things are "exceedingly good."[3] That includes me. That includes all of us.

Sometimes we just need to hear the truth of the Gospel over, and over, and over again for it to break through. We have so many defenses, so many lies shooting through our being. We need some truth reminding us who we really are. You are loved. No, really. You are loved. You are truly loved, even in the depths of your darkness.

LECTIO DIVINA

Bible quizzing was a popular activity for us growing up in the church. If you're not familiar with bible quizzing, it involves memorizing large portions of scripture and competing against others to see who can recite them better. It could be fun, but also competitive and stressful. There are many passages of scripture that I know because of quizzing, so I benefited greatly from the experience. Yet, it also reveals a sometimes unhealthy approach to scripture.

We often treat the Bible like a textbook, and end up consuming it for information that can be recited rather than a message of healing and transformation. For a long time I have had a strong memory of what was written in scripture. If you were looking for the location of a particular passage, I could probably find it for you. The problem was that much of it did not break through the blockade of defensive mechanisms surrounding my soul.

When I was struggling with how to understand my faith, I could barely stand to open the Bible, let alone extensively study it as I had done before. I decided to approach it a different way. I had learned about an approach to scripture in college known as *lectio divina*. Essentially it involves reading manageable passages of scripture, usually around four or five verses, so that one can meditate and contemplate the meaning. I mostly ignored this method in college because I was so obsessed with being the most knowledgeable student I could be. Now I was desperate to try a more intimate approach.

This way of approaching scripture involves reading the chosen passage slowly several times and observing if certain words stand out. We then take time to meditate on the passage. This is not so much analyzing the passage as it is simply sitting with it and trusting for the Spirit to illuminate the words within you. Often, out of this the desire to speak to God arises, sometimes to thank him for what he is telling us, or asking him to continue

---

3. Ware, *Orthodox Way*, 743.

to light our path. The last step is contemplation, or simply praying through silence.

The passage that has probably gripped me more than any other within this practice is Matthew 11: 28-30, particularly from The Message. I've referenced it before, but it's so good, so here it is again:

> "Are you tired? Worn out? Burned out on religion? Come to me. Get away with me and you'll recover your life. I'll show you how to take a real rest. Walk with me and work with me—watch how I do it. Learn the unforced rhythms of grace. I won't lay anything heavy or ill-fitting on you. Keep company with me and you'll learn to live freely and lightly."

At one time I could read this passage and casually dismiss its significance. "Sure, God wants to give us rest. Yeah I know, I get it." As I took time to focus on this one passage, it started to seep in, like God was my personal therapist repeating these lines to me. Over and over, for months even, I read this passage exclusively, and it slowly penetrated my soul.

I began to realize that my entire life was all about forcing it. I pretended around people so much. I even pretended with myself. It was painful and soothing at the same time. I didn't know what it was like to live in a way where my thoughts, words, and actions flowed from a secure place within me. To be honest, I would never have imagined this was even possible. I had so many heavy burdens laid on me, many of them self-inflicted. Living was labored and exhausting. I had heard people speak of living by the Spirit, but I had no clue what that looked like. Frankly, based on their harsh religious language, perhaps many of them didn't know what it looked like either. "Are you tired? Worn out? Burned out on religion?" Yes, yes, and yes.

I don't want to give the impression that my life is now smooth and easy, or that I constantly live from a peaceful center that never wavers. That's not the case. I still get anxious and insecure at times. But I can tell you this: What God has done within me—bringing healing and relief—I never imagined was possible. It was just a pipe dream. I'm not finished, and yet I've come so far. This approach to scripture was a huge help in that.

CENTERING PRAYER

There is perhaps nothing more humbling, or humiliating, than silent prayer. There is a torrent of useless thoughts and wild emotions rushing inside of us. Even if the thoughts are important, we often have little control over how they direct us. Most of the time we are blind to all this. The busyness of life can keep us distracted. Take a moment of silence or solitude, however, and it will be abundantly clear. As Cynthia Bourgeault echoes, "You'll sit down on your cushion or prayer stool with the lofty intention of making yourself totally available to God, and not twenty seconds later you'll find yourself deeply embroiled in some mental or emotional scenario: replaying that argument you had with your boss yesterday or wondering what to cook for dinner tonight."[4]

That doesn't make silent prayer sound very appealing, does it? It's not, but it is immensely helpful. Once again, the first step is seeing we have a problem. Silent prayer is an effective way to begin noticing how little control we really have, even over ourselves.

It may not sound like it, but it's a good thing. It's a practical way to see how self-defeating our egos really are, and centering prayer provides a way to begin giving over control. We allow God to speak to the deepest parts, even the ones we're not aware of.

Centering prayer is a form of silent prayer that helps with this. It involves choosing a word that has some significance that we can return to when our thoughts run amuck, as they inevitably do.

As I mentioned before, my wife is a Californian, while I am a Midwestern boy. There were a few regional differences in our English dialects. The one that came to light the quickest was our respective words for a carbonated beverage. While I grew up referring to it as a "pop," Irene was used to calling it a "soda." We had several lively debates early in our relationship as to which term was correct. Of course, we both thought we were right.

Then one day I noticed that I had begun referring to it as "soda." Not only did I stop referring to it as "pop," but even saying that felt weird and foreign to me. Now, whenever we visit the Midwest and hear people calling it "pop," it jolts me a little. I'll forget that I even used to call it that as well.

This shift never came in a dramatic fashion. Irene never demanded that I start using her term. I never formally made the decision to stop saying "pop." It just happened. Over time, being in relationship with Irene had an impact on me, and I had an impact on her. We are who we are today in part because of the influence we have had on each other. This didn't mainly happen in life altering moments; it happened in subtle ways, and we were oblivious to them most of the time.

This is how prayer works much of the time as well. We may not notice any dramatic moments for a bit, but then one day we are struck by how slow we are to become angry, or how quickly we let go of bitterness. What goes on in the deepest moments of prayer is mysterious to us. As Cynthia

4. Bourgeault, *Centering Prayer*, 17.

Bourgeault assures us, "You're in the right ballpark if your intention is "to be totally open to God": totally available, all the way down to that innermost point of your being; deeper than your thinking, deeper than your feelings, deeper than your memories and desires, deeper than your usual psychological sense of yourself."[5]

Sometimes the best way to be with another is to simply be present with no words, activity, or agenda. We don't want to do that very often. It can feel uncomfortable, or even frightening. Over time, however, it will become more natural, and the present won't seem so empty.

That's what this is all about: encountering the presence of God all around us, especially in the times and localities where we thought this was impossible. Even there we are pleasantly surprised and saying, like Jacob, "God is in this place—truly. And I didn't even know it!"[6]

5. Ibid, 17.
6. Gen 28:16 (MSG).

Chapter 20

A Healing Moment for Jesus

CHRISTIANS CONFESS THAT JESUS Christ is the Son of God, but often overlook his humanity. In reality, Jesus's most frequent term for himself was son of man, or "son of a human one." Jesus wanted people to know that he was like them. He was human, but even more so than us. We usually speak of Jesus as if our conclusion must be that he was capable of a life we could only dream of. On the contrary, Jesus came to show us how to be the people God created us to be.

There were some in the early church who would diminish Jesus's humanity. This assertion formed into a view referred to as *docetism*, which comes from the word, "to seem." Thus the belief was that Jesus was God, but only appeared to be human. The result is that we cannot hope to live the life that Jesus lived. It also strongly implies that divinity can have no real transforming effect on our flesh and blood humanity. The early church formerly recognized this as heretical because it short changes what God offers us.[1]

In reality, Jesus was a real flesh and blood human being. He had to use the facilities like everyone else. Occasionally he felt under the weather.

There was something else Jesus would have shared with us: pain. Jesus would have dealt with emotional turmoil at times. He would learn, as we all do, to navigate hormones, ups, and downs he encountered to become more emotionally mature. And like us, severe emotional pain from trauma or disturbing experiences and images would have stuck with him. Difficult

---

1. To specify, labeling a teaching as heretical is not a way to label the one teaching it as stupid or inferior. It is simply saying that the Gospel has beauty, grace, and power to it, and the heretical teaching is shortchanging the message. As a professor of mine used to say, any heresy is such because it misses out on the scope of God's love.

experiences in childhood can leave lasting impact, and Jesus would have had plenty.

I'm not suggesting that Jesus had a difficult or painful home life. By all accounts Mary and Joseph were very loving parents. Jesus did, however, have a unique beginning with the virgin birth. We often think of our modern selves as knowledgeable and intelligent versus ancient people as primitive and ignorant. People in Jesus day may not have known about DNA and atoms, but they knew about the birds and the bees. They knew that a particular activity preceded pregnancy. Thus, if anyone knew Jesus and his family and knew of the virgin story, they would likely have had the same reaction we would have.

Some close to Mary were sympathetic to her story, like her husband, Joseph, and her cousin, Elizabeth. Most people in their community would not have been, and this would have had difficult consequences for Jesus. Michael Hardin explains, "It is important to know that as Jesus grew up, his mamzer or bastard status would have prevented him from participating in the Temple cult. Jesus knew what it was like not to be able to share in the privilege of worshipping God as other Jewish males. For those who knew him, Jesus had a questionable paternity that would have had severe social consequences. No one would betroth his or her daughter to him. He would have known what it was like to be excluded from the synagogue or Temple service. He knew what it was like to be a leper or a menstruating woman or someone with a wound that would not heal."[2]

In short, Jesus would have been persecuted or, at the very least, spoken about harshly because of his origins. There is also question about when his adoptive father, Joseph, passed away. Joseph is only mentioned by name around the birth stories, the escape to Egypt, and the return to Galilee. He was also present when Jesus sat among the teachers in the temple at age twelve. So Jesus had a human father in his life, but for how long we do not know.

Either way, Jesus would have noticed the leering looks from people in his community. He would have heard the talk. And as with any of us, especially as children, words would have had impact. Humans are mysterious creatures. There is a depth to our beings. We can experience a myriad of emotions at any one time. We can believe but, at the same time, be tempted toward despair.

By the time of Jesus's public ministry he seems to have a rock solid foundation for his identity in his Father. We often think, because Jesus was divine, that he would have had such issues nailed down immediately. We

2. Hardin, *Jesus Driven Life*, 1819.

picture him arriving on earth with a divine download about who he was, his mission, and what he would face. That's not the depiction we have in the Gospels, however. Instead, Jesus relies on the Spirit to speak to him, guide him, and strengthen him. The author of Hebrews goes so far as to say, "Although he was a Son, he learned obedience through what he suffered; and having been made perfect, he became the source of eternal salvation for all who obey him."[3] Jesus learned the way we all tend to learn: through difficulties, trials, and pain.

When Jesus was growing up, then, I wonder if there were times when thoughts creeped in and tempted him to give up. Would he have heard the slander? "There goes Jesus, you heard that he's illegitimate, right? No, Joseph's not his real father. His mother actually believes that he was conceived by God." Maybe, as Hardin suggests, he was excluded from certain religious practices and community customs. When we experience ridicule as children, it has a way of sticking with us. It can get triggered in a variety of ways and can have a crippling effect. I wonder if Jesus ever had those nagging thoughts growing up, like thoughts that attacked his identity. Perhaps Jesus, as a human being, faced the same questions that nag at us.

Imagine if some of those nagging thoughts were still hanging around as he is approaching his public ministry. Maybe some of those scars and hurtful words as a child still stick with him. Deep down, however, he believes that his Father is leading him in this direction. So he decides to literally take the plunge and be baptized by his cousin, John the Baptist. Imagine all the jabs about where he came from, who his father was, and the persecution that would come from all of it. Imagine daring to believe that your Father has called upon you to lead disciples and to challenge religious authorities when many excluded you from even participating with them in worship. And then, as Jesus is lifted from the water, beads rolling off his head, he hears this message from the voice of God. "This is my Son, whom I love; with him I am well pleased."[4]

What relief, what soothing words to hear: "This is my Son." So many people doubted and ridiculed him. So many chided his family for their ridiculous assertion. While many would have argued that Jesus's origins signaled abandonment by God, the Father says otherwise. "This is my Son, and I love him."

As a man, it is hard to describe how meaningful and empowering it is to hear an older male whom I respect say the words, "I'm proud of you." I have so often doubted that there was anything good or worthwhile inside

3. Heb 5:8-9 (NRSV).
4. Matt 3:17 (NIV).

of me. I have been overwhelmed with shame, doubt, and self-loathing. I am fortunate enough to have had my father tell me, as I was leaving for college, "I'm proud of you. You deserve this." In the last conversation I had with my dear Grandpa Green, my heart swelled with joy as he doted on me, "I'm so proud of you, son." So when Jesus rose from the waters and heard his Father's voice, there was deep emotional healing that took place.

Jesus was given a point of assurance for his identity. I've encountered moments like that. I'm sure you have as well. Maybe it's through a moving song or a meaningful movie. Perhaps it came during a sunrise or a word from a loved one. It's a reminder that we are more than what we think; there's something powerful within us. It offers courage and hope. We have to fight to hold on, because soon thoughts of doubt and fear come to steal it away.

So it was with Jesus. Along comes the enemy. When we refer to the devil, we often see images of the red guy with horns and a pitch fork. This is not what scripture is conveying. Satan is not so much a name as much as it is a title that means "the accuser." We all know what the accuser feels like. Sometimes it comes through self-doubt, anxiety, depression, or shame, but it is that spirit which seeks to divide and tear us down.

In the same way, it does so with Jesus. He has just experienced this amazing moment of affirmation from his Father, and in comes that harassing voice, "Are you really the Son of God? Maybe you're not. Just to make sure, why don't you make some bread from stone? No one will believe you unless you can prove it."

The Satan, the accuser, tries to engage our insecurities, our ego, or what many spiritual instructors call the "false self." It is the self that believes we need to achieve, please, and impress in order to have a sense of identity. I've spent a large portion of my life agonizing over what people think of me. I also am prone to assuming that others have it all together and to becoming envious because I tend to feel deficient.

But just as there is a false self, there is also a true self. The true self is the self that God created. It is the self that exists solely and completely because of his love. While the false self strives to prove itself, the true self can relax and be content; it knows all that it desires has already been given, that it is already "exceedingly good," as Ware writes.

The false self, on the other hand, has no foundation, and deep down it knows. That's why it overcompensates. It is always wondering what's next and where it is in the ladder of success, whatever success looks like in a particular situation. When it fails, the ego either resorts to self-promotion or self-debasement. It seeks to find validity outside of itself, and these are the only responses it knows when failure inevitably occurs.

Jesus shows us where our foundation comes from. It comes from knowing that we are unconditionally loved. It comes from the fact that the creator of our universe thinks fondly of us, even when we don't know how to think well of ourselves. It is an identity that is enduring and unchanging. Our participation and realization of that fact, however, can change, often when we are distracted and overwhelmed by the action and chaos around us.

This is why Jesus was always going to "lonely places" to be alone with his Abba. One such example shows that the disciples didn't understand his behavior:

"Very early in the morning, while it was still dark, Jesus got up, left the house and went off to a solitary place, where he prayed. Simon and his companions went to look for him, and when they found him, they exclaimed: 'Everyone is looking for you!'"[5]

We often forget that Jesus depended on the Spirit just as we do. He relished the love of his Father and thus did not put stock in the opinions that others had of him. "I'm not interested in crowd approval,"[6] he told the religious leaders. Or as John put it, "Jesus would not entrust himself to them, for he knew all people. He did not need any testimony about mankind, for he knew what was in each person."[7]

Jesus knew his identity, and his life seamlessly flowed accordingly, so much so that he spoke as though his life depended on staying faithful to it. In response to the devil tempting him to make bread out of stones, Jesus responded, "One does not live by bread alone, but by every word that comes from the mouth of God."[8]

On another occasion, the disciples tried to get Jesus to take a lunch break. He responded, "I have food to eat that you know nothing about . . . my food," said Jesus, "is to do the will of him who sent me and to finish his work."[9]

So much of that work involved showing love and compassion to the oppressed and unloved among his people. Jesus could sympathize with them because of persecution he likely experienced in his childhood. He could look compassionately into the eyes of the woman who had been bleeding for years because he knew what it was to be outcast for something he could not

---

5. Mark 1:35-37 (NIV).
6. John 5:41 (MSG).
7. John 2:24-25 (NIV).
8. Matt 4:4 (NRSV).
9. John 4:32, 34 (NRSV).

control. He could understand the pain of the lepers and sinners because he too had been viewed as unfit.

Our scars and wounds are the things we typically think make us deficient. Instead, they are the marks that help us see the world compassionately.

Jesus was willing to enter the pain, all the way to the cross. We are far less willing. To get there, we must meet our ending point; that's really the only way to take that journey. At that point it's the only option we have. When we finally venture in, we find God making something profoundly beautiful.

Paul Young demonstrates this so deeply in *The Shack* through the journey of the main character. Mack's pain and suffering is concentrated in the shack where his daughter was brutally murdered. It's the last place he wants to go, which means it's precisely where he needs healing. Thus, God leads him there to move forward. We don't like it, but that's usually how it works.

As we journey on, we can trust that Jesus can walk with us intimately because he has entered the darkness himself. As Hebrews puts it, in Peterson's words, Jesus is not "out of touch with our reality. He's been through weakness and testing, experienced it all—all but the sin. So let's walk right up to him and get what he is so ready to give. Take the mercy, accept the help."[10]

10. Heb 4:15-16 (MSG).

Chapter 21

A New Kind of Love

I CAN BE A very competitive person, oftentimes to a fault. To give you an idea, my wife refused to play certain board games with me for years because I was sometimes not a very pleasant teammate. I would also get embarrassingly angry at times when I played and lost video games. There's a balance when we're playing a game or trying to grow in a particular activity. We want to have a challenge so that we improve. If the challenge is so extensive that we always feel crushed, however, it can make us lose our motivation to keep playing.

But some games, no matter how hard we try, are simply unbeatable. People pleasing is one of those games. I grew up in a church culture that was obsessed with people's opinions about us. In dysfunctional church world, appearance is king. We could not do anything that would raise questions or invite suspicion, even if the reason for the ensuing chastisement was that people were being ignorant and closed minded.

That was my world. Then I became a pastor myself. As you can expect, that did not help things. I even had a professor tell us, in all seriousness, that we needed to be better than everyone else in order to avoid criticism. It should be no surprise, then, that pastors have such a high burnout rate.

People pleasing can easily be mistaken for love. Jesus tells us to love each other, but we often miss the part about loving them as ourselves. That is, we can't love someone very well—whether that be a neighbor, friend, or significant other—if we are psychologically and emotionally dependent on him or her for our survival. The church misses this, but to be fair, most of our culture misses it as well. Most romantic movies are based on the narrative that love is about needing each other to survive. This is often seen as a sign that two people belong together, but it can also be a warning sign of deeper issues.

I know of what I speak, not because I've mastered relationships, but because I've fallen into all the aforementioned traps. That was one of the pitfalls in the early years of our marriage. We were both struggling with our own individual difficulties, and we thought we were meant to be the resolution for each other. It filled us with immense pressure and stress, and it made us feel like failures when we apparently weren't doing our jobs very well. Thankfully we both had a light-bulb moment when our marriage counselor enlightened us, "You cannot be everything to each other."

Our society is built on being obsessed with what others think of us. Just look at how the marketing and advertisements subtly, or not so subtly, inform us that our lives are simply not complete without their product and service. Don't take their word for it; however, listen to the celebrity or sports star's testimony. We talk about how ridiculous these commercials are; and yet, they must be working for the profits to keep growing.

Our concept of love can look very dissimilar to Jesus. Christians believe that Jesus embodied love and compassion, and yet he could tell people that he didn't care one iota about their approval. That seems harsh to someone immersed in a people-pleasing universe. But as we saw last chapter, Jesus could love, and care, and serve people precisely because he put no stock in their opinions of him. His service came from a place of genuine concern, not neurotic worrying about how he would be perceived.

We often find this mode of existence challenging. We can be blind to our motives because we don't know how much our pain distorts the way we live. A kind word to another person can become an attempt to earn affection. A favor given can become a subtle way to buy loyalty. We all have our manipulations. We can be blind to the storm whirling within us, and in turn become consumed with easing our pain, sometimes at the expense of other people.

When we are distracted or oblivious to our interior world, our actions usually end up stemming from all the pain and discomfort inside. As we discussed earlier, the way to let go is not by pushing things aside, but by embracing them just as God does. We're not very adept at this, however, so our actions usually are motivated by a hope that the person across from us can bring the healing and relief that we haven't been able to locate anywhere else. This results in codependency, resentment when the other person doesn't come through, and deeper insecurity.

When I was in college, a professor shared a message with us about the nature of love. He described what love usually looks like for us, especially when we're young and first learning the art of relationships. In this first stage, we love as the person does what we desire him or her to do for us. I love people if they fulfill the expectations I have for them. Many marriages begin this way as young partners are unaware that they have expectations at all.

Hopefully most of us move past this stage, where our love is the result of how the person impacts us. I love someone because she makes me feel secure, or because she is a lovely presence, or because she doesn't get annoyed at my obsession with *Star Wars*. This is slightly better than the first stage, but it's still focused on what I get out of the relationship. It also views love as a feeling resulting from what someone does for me.

Because both of these modes of love are focused on what I get, they can lead toward codependency. When we love someone for what we get out of the relationship, it can lead to fear of losing that person. Now, we all would be devastated to lose a loved one. That's not what I'm talking about. If we think we cannot survive without another person, our love for him or her can become self-serving and even manipulative. Once again we become our own worst enemies.

These "attachments" have been recognized as barriers to spiritual health across many religious traditions. Jesus seems to be addressing this when he instructed, "If you try to hang on to your life, you will lose it. But if you give up your life for my sake, you will save it. And what do you benefit if you gain the whole world but lose your own soul? Is anything worth more than your soul?"[1] When we cling to our attachments, convinced we need them to be happy, we end up pushing down our true selves. Even when we obtain what we were chasing, the inner security we thought it would bring eludes us. This type of attachment has the "power to thrill you when you attained it, to make you anxious lest you be deprived of it and miserable when you lose it."[2]

I fell into this trap in the early years of our marriage. Though Irene had said "I do," I was afraid that she would see too deeply within me and reject me. Because of this, I guarded myself to the point that she felt as though she didn't really know me. When we had conversations, I would often respond diplomatically instead of honestly. In this way I used manipulation to keep her at a distance in order to preserve the relationship. It's backward and self-sabotaging, but these are the types of dysfunctional behaviors that form out of repressed shame.

This is why learning to live and find security in our true identities is so important. If we don't walk that journey, we will not be able to love others as ourselves. Our culture would have us believe that loving means not being able to live without the other. In reality, if we cannot live without someone,

1. Matt 16:25-26 (NLT).
2. De Mello, *Way to Love*, 16.

we won't be able to truly love him or her. Our attempts at love will instead be endeavors at self-preservation.

To truly be able to love, we have to encounter the same love and acceptance that Jesus encountered and stood upon each moment of his life. Jesus was loved and adored by his Father, but it doesn't end with him. Jesus invites us into this love as well. Invite might not even be strong enough. He accomplishes this union and leads us to recognize this reality. We don't have to make this connection happen. We are already united with God, through Christ. What's missing is awareness and acceptance of that reality. Thus, David Benner affirms, "Personhood is not an accomplishment; it is a gift . . . our true self-the self we are becoming in God-is something we receive from God. Any other identity is an illusion."[3]

Jesus invites us to live in the truth, and challenges our futile attempts at living outside of it. In one of his more confusing and worrisome statements, Jesus declared, "Whoever comes to me and does not hate father and mother, wife and children, brothers and sisters, yes even life itself, cannot be my disciple. Whoever does not carry the cross and follow me cannot be my disciple."[4]

If this passage makes you cringe a bit, you're not the only one. But we must remember, once again, that Jesus was a prophet. As such, he often used fantastic sayings or hyperbolic language to make a point. Jesus is speaking about the control we frequently let others have over our lives. This happens when we become dependent on their affection or approval for our happiness. Clearly receiving affection from a loved one is a beautiful thing, but if our happiness depends on it, we are asking too much of that person and will be disappointed when she cannot be everything to us.

What Jesus is saying is that unless we've tasted the bitterness of being twisted and pulled by every expectation of those around us, we won't be ready to embrace the fullness of our identity in him. I survived so long by trying to fulfill the expectations of others. My desire for their approval dictated my every move like a marionette. Only when I was faced with how controlled I really was could I even begin to hope that another way was possible.

That is why Jesus leads us to the cross, to our pain and struggles—so we can see the ways we depend on outside forces for our happiness. The truth is that there are people in this world exuding joy who don't have the conveniences, the material blessings, or the safety from suffering that we do. They have suffered much; and yet, in a profound way their suffering has

3. Benner, *Gift of Being Yourself,* 45.

4. Luke 14:26-27 (NRSV).

brought them to an illuminating truth: they don't need anything else to be happy.

Jesus is offering us a different vantage point to love from, and that point is abundance. There is an abundance of that which we truly desire: love, joy, peace, and contentment. Many who have suffered have seen this more clearly because all that we think we need has been stripped away, but the true treasures remain.

That's what the father communicates to the older son in the parable of the prodigal. The older son has slaved away all his life waiting to get what was his. His father enlightens him, "You are always with me, and everything I have is yours."[5] Imagine the possibilities if we could come to a place where we truly believe in that reality. We are always with him, and everything he has is ours.

Peter tells his readers, as Peterson paraphrases it, "Since Jesus went through everything you're going through and more, learn to think like him." Then he continues, "Think of your sufferings as a weaning from that old sinful habit of always expecting to get your own way. Then you'll be able to live out your days free to pursue what God wants instead of being tyrannized by what you want."[6]

We try so hard to control the situations we're in or the people that we're around, thinking all that maneuvering will bring us peace and rest. That kind of rest usually only lasts for a moment, if at all. All the while we're consumed with preventing the next catastrophe. The truth is we are so often tyrannized by what we want because it's out of a sense of insecurity. If we lived out of abundance, we would realize that what we most long for is already true: we are loved, we are accepted, and we belong. Then our thoughts, desires, and actions can come from a more secure place.

When we learn to live from abundance, we discover what we have to offer the world, and what we can delight in with others. We are deeply impacted by each other, and when relationships exist in freedom, we can allow our individual expressions of humanity to combine and create a beautiful dynamic that would otherwise not exist. I can acknowledge the gift of my personhood, and also the blessing that your presence offers.

When we discover our true selves, we discover the beauty inside us, the same beauty in others as beloved children of God. It's a humbling discovery, and a liberating one. The beauty of it doesn't depend on you or me. It just is. I now have something to offer. It's not enhanced by my successes or diminished by my screw ups. This is the truth that gives us the freedom we need to love.

5. Luke 15:31 (NIV).
6. 1 Pet 4:1-2 (MSG).

CHAPTER 22

Jesus Goes the Distance

WHEN I WAS LITTLE, probably around five years old, we had neighbors behind our house who had an adorable black dog. He was so fluffy and cuddly. I loved that dog. One day our neighbors made a passing remark that did not pass by my notice. "You can play with him anytime," they said, "just think of him as your dog too." They did not realize how literal I would take that. The next day I went over to see my new dog. I pet him and played with him, and since he was now my dog, I unhooked him from his leash in their backyard and brought him home. My parents were mortified, the neighbors were upset, and I was confused. After all, they said he was my dog.

Kids have that sense of innocence and belief that makes them interpret reality around them in such a sincere way. As I mentioned before, I have worked for a school district for the last several years. I love watching the kids, especially the little ones, and the hilarious things they do. It's quite entertaining. It's also refreshing, because we often lose that sense of joy and spontaneity. Pain and difficulties happen, and they can lead us to make negative assumptions about ourselves and the world around us. It becomes the driving story to our lives. If we are full of shame and see ourselves as rotten and flawed, it will impact our mental landscape, even to the point of how we remember the past.

Can you see why our starting point for our identities is so important— not just in our mental landscapes, but also in the way we understand our faith and what it says about us? Do we start in the beginning, where God created us in his image and said we were good? Or do we start with the fall and see our base identities as corrupt?

My father was like most fathers when I was younger. He loved me, but in moments of stress or anger he could be . . . not himself. I understand that

173

intimately because there are times when I am not myself either and react to loved ones in short or grumpy ways. There were also times when my father's love for me would come out clearly in his own unique way.

One of those times was after a Little League baseball game. I was a fast base runner and a pretty good hitter, but my defense was lacking. I would sometimes get nervous when the ball was hit toward me. This particular game, however, I had several fly balls hit my way, and I caught them all.

I was very excited, and on our way to the car after the game, I asked my dad, "Did you see me catch those fly balls?"

"Yep, you did good out there."

Then I asked him the question that every son is dying to know. "Are you proud of me?"

My dad, in his own quirky way, gave me the best response, "Oh, you could try to catch the ball with your teeth, and I'd still be proud of you." In other words, it is not what you do, but your identity as my son that makes me proud of you.

That's one of the best moments I've ever had with my dad. The problem was that for years I completely forgot about it. When I did remember it, I kept it in the background. Why? Because it didn't fit my self-narrative. It didn't fit what I believed about myself, or how I believed God saw me.

Objectively, this moment with my dad is much more reflective of how he felt about me than the times where he was stressed, angry, or overwhelmed. I had built a self-narrative, however, out of interactions with family, with friends, and what I believed about God and his opinion of me.

This has begun to change, but only as I allowed Jesus to lead me into my darkness. I was so terrified at what I would find. I had determined to keep it buried for the rest of my life. At least then I could pretend it didn't exist. That would be much preferable to finding out that all my deepest fears were confirmed.

I finally accepted his invitation to sit with my skeletons, more out of a sense of desperation than anything else. I discovered that most of what I had been terrified of was a lie I was believing about myself and God. The veil was stripped away. The stuff that had been true paled in significance to the loving embrace of Abba. I had lived an interior nightmare for so long. It was an incredibly painful journey, but Jesus took me down to the depths so I could rise with him to new life.

This is not really an ending but a new beginning. I have a long journey to continue. The difference is that I have a new starting point. Instead of seeing myself as flawed or rejected, I have a new vantage point. I can hear my dad saying he will be proud of me no matter what, and start to grasp it as my story. I can recall the Father saying of Jesus, "This is my Son, whom I love, with him I am well pleased," and begin to believe that it is true of me as well. I cannot adequately describe how huge a step that is for me.

I had just poured out all my garbage to my spiritual director, and he assured me that neither he nor any of the saints were better than me. We all have baggage. "I love Jesus more than I ever have," I told him, "because I've seen to what lengths he'll go to rescue me."

He smiled effortlessly, the way someone smiles when they relate intimately to what you're saying. "He always goes the distance," he affirmed.

I have a new sense of my identity, and it begins with Jesus's message to his disciples, "You will know that I am in my Father, and you in me, and I in you."[1] No one is strong enough to change that.

My hope is that by your desire to move forward, or your desperation no longer to stay where you are, you will journey with Jesus into the depths of your soul. May you find the God in your closet embracing your darkest skeletons. May you learn acceptance of yourself and the transformation that follows. And may you begin to see with new eyes . . . that you are in him, and he is in you. Trust him; he will always go the distance.

1. John 14:20 (NRSV).

Bibliography

"Babylonian Talmud: Tractate Berakoth." http://www.come-and-hear.com/berakoth_55. htm.

Bauckham, Richard. "The Language of Warfare in the Book of Revelation." In *Compassionate Eschatology: The Future as Friend*, edited by Ted Grimsrud and Michael Hardin, 28–41. Eugene, OR: Cascade, 2011. (Kindle Edition)

Beilby, James, and Eddy, Paul R., eds. *The Nature of the Atonement: Four Views*. Downers Grove, IL: IVP Academic, 2009.

Bell, Rob. *What Is the Bible: How an Ancient Library of Poems, Letters, and Stories Can Transform the Way You think and Feel About Everything*. New York: Harper One, 2017. (Kindle Edition)

Benner, David G. *The Gift of Being Yourself: The Sacred Call to Self-Discovery*. Westmont, IL: IVP, 2004.

Bourgeault, Cynthia. *The Heart of Centering Prayer: Nondual Christianity in Theory and Practice*. Boulder: Shambhala, Inc. 2016. (Kindle Edition)

Chrysostom, John. "The Easter Sermon of John Chrysostom." http://anglicansonline. org/special/Easter/chrysostom_easter.html.

De Mello, Anthony. *The Way to Love: The Last Meditations of Anthony De Mello*. New York: Doubleday, 1992.

Enns, Peter. *Inspiration and Incarnation: Evangelicals and the Problem of the Old Testament*. Grand Rapids: Baker Academic, 2015. (Kindle Edition)

Flood, Derek. *Disarming Scripture: Cherry-Picking Liberals, Violence-Loving Conservatives, and Why We All Need to Learn to Read the Bible Like Jesus Did*. San Francisco: Metanoia, 2014. (Kindle Edition)

——. *Healing the Gospel: A Radical Vision for Grace, Justice, and the Cross*. Eugene, OR: Cascade, 2012. (Kindle Edition)

Freeman, Curtis W. "The Faith of Jesus Christ: An Evangelical Conundrum." In *Beyond Old and New Perspectives on Paul: Reflections on the Work of Douglas Campbell*, edited by Chris Tilling, 6283–6440. Eugene, OR: Cascade, 2014. (Kindle Edition)

Goleman, Daniel. *Emotional Intelligence: Why it can matter more than IQ*. New York: Bantam, 1995.

Grimsrud, Ted. "Biblical Apocalyptic: What Is Being Revealed?" In *Compassionate Eschatology: The Future as Friend*, edited by Ted Grimsrud and Michael Hardin, 3–27. Eugene, OR: Cascade, 2011. (Kindle Edition)

Hardin, Michael. *The Jesus Driven Life: Reconnecting Humanity With Jesus*. Lancaster, PA: JDL, 2013. (Kindle Edition)

Heim, S. Mark. *Saved From Sacrifice: A Theology of the Cross*. Grand Rapids: Eerdmans, 2006.

Jacobsen, Wayne. *Finding Church: What If There Really Is Something More?* Newbury Park, CA: Trailview, 2014. (Kindle Edition)

Jersak, Brad. "Free Will, the Nous and Divine Judgment: A Critical Analysis of Three Visions of Universalism." *Christianity Without the Religion* (May 2014). https://christianity-without-the-religion.blogspot.com/2014/05/free-will-nous-and-divine-judgment.html.

———. *Her Gates Will Never Be Shut: Hope, Hell, and the New Jerusalem*. Eugene, OR: Wipf and Stock, 2009. (Kindle Edition)

———. *A More Christlike God: A More Beautiful Gospel*. Pasadena: Plain Truth Ministries, 2015. (Kindle Edition)

Julian of Norwich. *Revelations of Divine Love*. Overland Park, KS: Digireads, 2013. (Kindle Edition)

Johnson, Raborn. "Compassionate Eschatology with Michael Hardin". *Beyond the Box*, Podcast audio, Feb. 1, 2012. http://www.beyondtheboxpodcast.com/2012/02/compassionate-eschatology-with-michael-hardin.

MacDonald, Gregory. *The Evangelical Universalist*. Eugene, OR: Cascade, 2012. (Kindle Edition)

Mathewes-Green, Frederica. *The Illumined Heart: Capture the Vibrant Heart of the Ancient Christians*. Orleans, MA: Paraclete, 2007.

"The Nicene Creed." http://anglicansonline.org/basics/nicene.html.

Pasquale, Teresa B. *Sacred Wounds: A Path to Healing from Spiritual Trauma*. St. Louis: Chalice, 2015. (Kindle Edition)

Plato. *The Republic*. Translated by Benjamin Jowett. (Kindle Edition)

Rhor, Richard. *Breathing Under Water: Spirituality and the Twelve Steps*. Cincinnati: St. Anthony Messenger, 2011. (Kindle Edition)

———. *Falling Upward: A Spirituality for the Two Halves of Life*. San Francisco: Jossey-Bass, 2011. (Kindle Edition)

———. *Things Hidden: Scripture as Spirituality*. Cincinnati: St. Anthony Messenger, 2008. (Kindle Edition)

"Selected Liturgical Hymns." https://oca.org/orthodoxy/prayers/selected-liturgical-hymns.

Singer, Merrill. *The Face of Social Suffering: The Life History of a Street Drug Addict*. Long Grove. IL: Waveland, 2006.

Tickle, Phyllis. *The Great Emergence: How Christianity Is Changing and Why*. Grand Rapids: Baker, 2012. (Kindle Edition)

Ware, Kallistos. "Dare We Hope for the Salvation of All?" *Clarion Journal of Spirituality and Justice* (February 2015). https://www.clarion-journal.com/clarion_journal_of_spirit/2015/02/dare-we-hope-for-the-salvation-of-all-kallistos-ware.html

———. *The Orthodox Way*. Crestwood, NY: St Vladimir's Seminary, 1979. (Kindle Edition)

Wesley, John. "Sermon 128." *Global Ministries The United Methodist Church* (1872) Part VII, section 2. https://www.umcmission.org/Find-Resources/John-Wesley-Sermons/Sermon-128-Free-Grace

Wood, Ralph C. "In Defense of Disbelief." *First Things*. (October 1998). https://www.firstthings.com/article/1998/10/002-in-defense-of-disbelief

Young, WM. Paul. *The Shack: When Tragedy Confronts Eternity*. Los Angeles: Windblown, 2007.

Zhand, Brian. *Sinners in the Hands of a Loving God: The Scandalous Truth of the Very Good News*. Colorado Springs: Waterbrook, 2017. (Kindle Edition)